antha **Collett** is a successful property investor with a e portfolio spanning the UK. She achieved early financial cess from property and is now a full-time investor. Samantha is the author of *How to Buy Property at Auction* writes a column in the *Evening Standard Homes & Property*. She regularly shares her property stories in her ti-award-winning blog What Sam Saw Today, which been featured in the *Telegraph* Top 10 property blogs. Samantha founded and later sold Gorgeous Homes, a perty lettings business, and has won the prestigious NLA Women in Property award.

Property Investment: The Essential Rules

How to use property to achieve
financial freedom and security

Samantha Collett

Constable & Robinson Ltd
55–56 Russell Square
London WC1B 4HP
www.constablerobinson.com

First published in the UK by How to Books,
an imprint of Constable & Robinson Ltd, 2014

A copy of the British Library Cataloguing in Publication
Data is available from the British Library

ISBN: 978-1-84528-584-5 (paperback)
ISBN: 978-1-84528-585-2 (ebook)

1 3 5 7 9 10 8 6 4 2

Printed and bound by CPI Group (UK) Ltd, Croydon, CR0 4YY

CONTENTS

ACKNOWLEDGEMENTS

No book is written in isolation. Unseen to the outside world are hours upon hours of debates, discussions and sparks of inspiration. I am especially grateful to Dimitris for his unwavering belief, love and support in me – plus his fantastic editorial feedback. I am thankful for my family and friends who continue to amaze me with their constant love and care. Special thanks are due to Jo King, Ruth Partlett and Jason Emmett, whose critical analysis and enthusiasm helped me shape, refine and better my work – and who provided continual encouragement and motivation. Thanks are also due to Nick Dare for sharing his Rules, and to my wonderful network of property friends who are a bedrock of support and source of inspiration.

Over the years I have talked with many property investors who, I am sure, have inadvertently influenced my Rules. I have also had the pleasure of managing countless tenancies and dealing with many agents, tradespeople and industry folk who have shaped my thinking, practices – and ultimately my Rules. I would like to thank them very much.

Finally, I would like to thank Nikki and Giles for giving me the opportunity to share my Rules.

INTRODUCTION

The beauty of property investment is its *inclusiveness*. It doesn't matter who you are, what education you have or job you do – *you* can make property investment your own business.

What path you choose to follow in your investment career is very much up to you. Property comes in all sorts of shapes and sizes and suits a variety of different needs and budgets. You may invest in Buy-to-Let, have a go at some development projects, or even take a chance on some future planning gains or speculative opportunities. Although I would counter, whatever route you take, there are some key principles you need to take on board; I call these *The Essential Rules*.

I've pondered a lot if I am the right person to write *Property Investment: The Essential Rules*. The main reason I questioned myself was because I have not had a perfect career. I have made mistakes, bought duds, and – gasp – even *lost* money in property. But I have also *made* money and have built a cash-flowing and healthy property portfolio that has enabled me to ditch the day job. And so, despite and *in spite* of the mistakes I have made, I reckon I am qualified to write *Property Investment: The Essential Rules* because I have learned from when I got it wrong and from when I got it right; I have learned what to do – and also what *not* to do.

Understanding what works and what doesn't work means I am better placed to formulate investment strategies to understand what is key to success. *The Essential Rules* are not set in stone, but I can tell you they are the guiding principles that I use, and which have been the bedrock to my property career.

I have been fortunate to have survived and thrived during the biggest housing market crash in living history, and to keep my business and my sanity. At times it has been tough, and I know success cannot be taken for granted. But the difference between me and many other investors is that I am not blinded by the sex appeal of property. Yes, I love property, and yes, I am passionate about people and property. However, I have always been very clear that this is a business. Property investment *is* a business and for you to succeed you need to get this clear from the outset.

Loving what you do is fantastic. Being passionate about what you do is wonderful. Making money from a fantastic industry that you are passionate about is a dream come true. And, if this is your dream, then I can only wish the same for you too.

But I have to tell you now: it is not always plain sailing. It is not always smiles, laughter, joyfulness and choosing new kitchens. Property investment can be hard work and it can involve sacrifices and maybe even a few sleepless nights. But, if you are able to balance the rough with the smooth and know that not every day is a picnic, you may well be cut out for a career in property investment.

It is a career in which *you* will be in the driving seat. You will need to step up to the challenge and take on board that you are now the boss. This can be scary in the beginning; it's not that often you get the chance to take such control of your life, your career and your future. But if you've got some stamina, some willpower, a bit of wherewithal and the desire to make your life happen, then property investment could well be the choice for you.

I hope you find *Property Investment: The Essential Rules* helpful and I wish you luck in your exciting new adventure – and it *is* an adventure. You will learn things about yourself you never knew you were capable of. You will find reserves of money, energy and ingenuity that will flabbergast and amaze you. You may even, if you really want to roll up your sleeves, learn you've got some hidden practical talents you never knew you had!

A career in property investment will teach you so much more about yourself than you knew previously. And the reason for this is because it's such a *personal* business. Property really is personal. It doesn't matter how big or small you want to grow your business, your property investment business is a reflection of you.

So make sure when you look at your business that you like what you see – this is your life and your business and you can build and make it how you want.

You just need to follow some Rules.

So let's get you started.

HOW TO USE THIS BOOK

Property Investment: The Essential Rules has been designed to provide actionable advice to help you become a successful property investor. It covers the practical side of investment, as well as the emotional aspects and the actual business of facts and figures that you need to succeed. The individual Rule approach is intended for easier reading and allows you to focus on those Rules that are more relevant to you. The 'Go For It!' exercises at the end of each Rule are designed to inspire and motivate you into action. You will reap the most benefit from the Rules by *taking* action. Action, no matter how small, moves you forward; so always keep going and every day aim to create a little more momentum in your life.

The book has been divided into four sections: Personal Rules, Property Rules, Business Rules and Customer Rules. Each of these areas plays an important role when it comes to property investment success. I start with the Personal Rules, because how you approach property investment is critical, and this section explores the mind-set of an investor and looks at the outcomes you hope to achieve by investing in property. The Property Rules section focuses on the property selection criteria and looks at how you can choose investments that suit you. The Business Rules are the nuts and bolts of running a property business and concentrate on the commercial aspects of investment. The Customer Rules section looks at how you build relationships and the services you need to provide that will help you develop processes and practices to deal with people.

Property Investment: The Essential Rules will teach you the guiding principles to help you get the most out of property investment. But, to *really* get the most, *you* also need to take action. So make a promise to yourself now, before we begin, that you too are committed to making the most out of *you*.

Let's get going . . .

PART ONE: PERSONAL RULES

Being a successful property investor requires a different way of thinking, acting and living. Personal Rules are those for you and how you live your life and approach property investment. We all have our own standards for how we want to be and what we want to achieve, but there are some key cornerstones for thinking and acting to get where we want to be. Each of us is different and so how far these Rules apply to you will depend upon your situation. However, it is important to have guiding principles. The values and philosophies you hold can centre you, challenge you and ensure you are on course to being the best investor you can be.

So take the time to work on you, your Personal Rules, and let's get you started with being who and where you want to be.

Rule 1: Know your plan

Investing in property is about investing in your plan.

Before you invest in property you should know what it is you are trying to achieve. You need to have an end goal of what you want from property investment. This plan will guide your investment career and will ultimately dictate the sort of properties you buy, sell and rent. Each of us has access to different resources – some may have more time, others may have more money, and then some may have more technical skills. It is only by understanding what it is you have to offer and what it is you want to achieve that you can formulate a plan for going forwards.

So what's the plan?

Why are you investing in property? What are you trying to achieve and hoping to get in the end? How much time do you want to give? How much money do you want to invest? How involved do you want to be? Are you trying to ditch the day job? Do you want to top up your pension? Are you hoping to build a nest egg for the future?

All of these questions are about the *purpose* of your property investment. They are the *why* of what you're doing. And you need to be clear about what this is. Investing in property is about investing in your plan. There are millions of properties available to buy. Which ones will you choose and why?

And that is ultimately why you need to know your plan, because your plan will guide you to buy the right property for you. Your investment property may not be your intended home to live in, but it is an intended purchase to produce an end goal. Not every property is built the same and not every property will produce the same outcome – that is why property must be bought according to the plan you have.

If you want to ditch the day job, you'll have to buy a different sort of property should you want to build a pension fund for the future. Alternatively, investing as a sideline to a full-time job will most likely require a property that is relatively hassle-free. Or, if you have a load of cash, don't need the income but want a roaring capital return, you'll likely buy something completely different again.

There is no 'one-size-fits-all' when it comes to property investment, because each and every one of us has our own plan. You will have your own dreams and goals for what you are trying to achieve by investing. The key to achieving this is in knowing your own plan and what you are trying to do. Only then can you start by investing in the right property for you.

Go For It!

Make a plan. Write down what your purpose is for investing in property and add your financial goals. For example:

- I want to use property to supplement my income by £X per month within X years.
- I want to use property as my main income and earn £X per month within X years.
- I want to use property to increase my capital investment by £X within X years.

Rule 2: What's your exit route?

Your exit route fundamentally underpins
your plan both now and in the future.

It's easy to fall into the trap of thinking: 'I'll buy a property, make a million and then retire.' That's what so many books, newspapers and TV shows have told us over the years. But those were different days and nowadays it's not that easy to make money from property investment. Buying a property is not like buying a lottery ticket. You won't wake up one day to find you are a multi-millionaire. Being a property investor can make you a lot of money, but it's not get-rich-quick. And it requires work if you want to make serious bucks.

Knowing your exit route guides your investment plan. It may feel like I'm asking you to think about getting divorced on your wedding day – but everybody needs to be prepared for when the marriage has run its course. This means you need to enter into the investment process by knowing how, when and what you want to *get out*. For some, there may be no intention to sell any properties and the estate will be handed to their heirs. For others, a property may be kept until it reaches a certain capital value and then disposed of.

Your exit route will guide the sort of properties you choose to invest in. Buying a property to rent out for twenty years is very different to buying a property to refurbish and sell on for a profit within a year. Investing in a property to build a healthy income-stream is not the same as buying a property that will drastically increase in capital value. Each of these outcomes requires different inputs; varying levels of money, time, effort and energy. Much of these will be influenced by what you want to achieve in the end.

Knowing your exit route influences both your entry and also your subsequent investment journey. It will impact upon how you decide to own a property (e.g. personally, in a Limited Company); it will influence how you manage the finances (i.e. to repay the capital debt) and also how you manage the investment on an everyday basis (e.g. hands-on or via an agent).

Your exit route fundamentally underpins your plan both now and in the future. You need to know why you are investing, what you hope to achieve and how you are going to get out with your rewards. Think about what you want from property, how the investment will fit with your life – or potentially change your life. What you achieve at the end is determined by the start – and everybody needs to start somewhere. So start now by focusing on the end goal and your exit route to riches!

Go For It!

Sit down with a piece of paper and write down your exit route.

Rule 3: Ask for more

Ask more: get more.

The more you ask, the more you get. Ask more: get more.

It's that simple.

You know the saying: 'If you don't ask, you don't get.' It's just so true. So maybe you need to start by asking for what you want and then asking for *more* of what you want. And you'll be pleasantly surprised to learn: the more you ask, the easier it gets. The first hurdle is asking in the first place. This is what most people really struggle with: actually asking. Pride, embarrassment and shyness are all great excuses for not getting what you want. Congratulations on being a proud, embarrassed, shy person who doesn't get what they want. Feel good? No, I didn't think so. And so now you need to take the leap and become that person who gets what they want. That starts with asking.

So how do you ask for what you want? Well, it starts with thinking about what you want and then asking for it. I know this all sounds really simple, but it is. You just have to take a deep breath and ask. And I would advise that you ask very nicely, very politely and say please. And then smile. Even if you're on the phone, it's best to smile, as people can hear smiles down the line, even if they can't see them.

I know that sounds a bit simplistic: 'Just ask for what you want.' But it can't really be dressed up. Most people make this hard because they don't actually *ask* for what they want, so they don't *get* what they want. If everybody in this world went around asking for what they wanted, the world would be a far harder place for getting what you want, because everybody would be doing it. And that's the secret: most people do not ask. Most people are so damn scared of themselves, and of what other people may think, that they don't ask. They daren't. That makes it a whole lot easier for those of us (and that includes you now) who are brave enough to ask for what we want. Most people *don't* ask, and so, when people *do* ask, it's a real pleasure, a treat. It's like something different. And the reward for being different, most of the time, is to get what you want.

This Rule applies to everything in life. Not just property. It's about *you*. It's about your life and what you want out of it. It's about giving yourself the best chance to go where you want to go and be who you want to be. The only way of doing that is by starting at the beginning and knowing what you want. Then you can ask for precisely that. And then you can ask for some more, please. Yes, it will be hard the first few times and there will be some knockbacks and maybe even a little bit of embarrassment involved. But when the time comes and you do get what you want, you'll soon realise how easy it was and be thankful that you kept asking. And then you'll ask for more. Because in the end you'll get what you want. And until that day, you just need to keep asking: more please!

Go For It!

Next time you're in a restaurant and you order food, ask for some more – an extra helping, or sauce, or whatever it is you're ordering. Just ask for more (please) and see how easy it is to get more just by asking for more.

Rule 4: Know who you want to be

Property investment can and
does fit with you.

Just as properties are not built the same, nor are people. And it is people who invest in property. Right now, you need to know who you want to be. Knowing the sort of property investor you want to be is critical to ensuring you buy the right property for you and how you want to live your life. Not everyone wants to spend days, nights and weekends doing up properties and not everyone wants to deal with tenants. Knowing who you want to be involves thinking about how property investment will fit with you and your life. You need to question how much of your life you want to devote to being a property investor.

At this point, it is OK to admit to *not* wanting to spend much time as a property investor. There's nothing wrong with wanting an easy life, investing as a sideline and enjoying your present career. It is not a prerequisite of property investment that it is the *only* thing you can do, nor that it has to become a major part of your life. Being a property investor does not have to become a key definer of your identity, nor does it even have to be a description of what you do. Property investment can and does fit with you. And it is your decision *how much of you* you want to give to this.

Property investors come from all walks of life, from

successful multi-billionaire businesspeople to unemployed people and retirees. And with every person who invests in property, there is a different reason behind what they're doing and what it means to them. For the successful businessperson property investment may just be a way of investing the company profits, whereas for the unemployed person property investment may be a whole new career. Knowing who you want to be will define what you buy and how you manage your property investment.

For those who are hell bent on ditching the day job, property investment will take on a very different mantle. But even within this, there are differing shades as to how far you want to go and how much time and effort you are willing to spend. By knowing who you want to be, you will be able to define what property investment means to you. You will know the risks you are prepared to take, the rewards you want to gain and the amount of time, money and effort you are willing to put in. Ultimately, much of this is down to you. It is only by knowing *who* you want to be and *what* you want to achieve that you will properly be able to start investing in property to get the success you are planning for.

Go For It!

Decide how property investment fits with you and your life. How much of *you* do you want to give? Do you want it to be a hobby, a future cash pot or a new career?

Rule 5: You don't have to be a know-it-all

You need to learn to live with uncertainty.

People ask too much of themselves. They expect to be an expert on something before they have even done it. Thinking you need to know it all before you do anything will mean you do nothing. Nobody can know it all. There is no point in trying to know it all, all you can know is as much as you can . . . to make a decision. No decision you make will ever be perfect. Things change, ideas evolve and we as people decide we want to do things differently. All you can do is make the best decision at that point in time. Period.

You need to learn to live with uncertainty. You need to make it your best friend. You can't know everything, nor should you. But as long as you are willing to learn and to ask questions about the stuff you don't know, then you won't go far wrong. Property investment is not a magic art, nor is it rocket science; it is plainly and simply buying and selling properties. If you're good at it, you'll make some money; if you're not, you'll lose money.

Feeling scared is natural. Being in unknown or unfamiliar situations means you won't know what to do. But as long as you are prepared to learn, you will know what to do. If not, you will find someone else who knows what to do. All you have to keep in mind when you don't know what to do is that you will be able to find someone else who does. This is why you don't have to be a know-it-all.

It is important to know your strengths and what you are good at. We are not all built the same; where you might be very good at building brick walls, I may be very good at painting those walls. It's about matching your skills to the job at hand. And understanding where you need help, especially in those areas where you don't know. For example, I don't know electrics. My understanding goes as far as I plug something into the wall and it works. When it doesn't, I check the fuse box to make sure it's not blown and that all the switches are turned on. Then I draw a blank. That is the level of my knowledge. However, I know a good electrician, and he deals with anything more complicated. That's because I don't know how to.

And it's OK for me to *not* know this. It's also OK for me to carry on not being a know-it-all when it comes to electrics, because I know somebody who *does* know. And the same applies for plumbing matters, roofing issues, glazing trouble, and just about any other maintenance jobs you can think of around the home. Because those are not my forte – property repairs are not my specialist subject. I stick to what I do best (property investment) and I find other people to do what they do best (property maintenance). Know what you need to know, and for the rest find some other know-it-all who knows best!

Go For It!

Attend a talk on a new subject (check out meetup.com for ideas) and ask the host a question.

Rule 6: Don't stop before you start

Action is what separates those who do and those who dream.

Investing in property is enormously exciting, but it can also feel overwhelming. It involves a lot of money and requires you to take risks. It will also test your business skills in ways that may have not been challenged before. For many investors, there is a desire to know as much as possible before getting started. Knowledge is fantastic and you will need as much of it as possible. However, there comes a point when your quest for information is actually just a 'procrastination process' rather than the basis of a do-able action plan.

The only way you can *really* get started in property investment is to begin. It is that simple. Once the research has been done and the funds are in hand, there is no reason *not* to do it. Unless you don't want to, or decide it's not for you. Property investment is not without its problems and if you don't want to take any form of risk or have additional responsibility, then this is not for you.

But if you are prepared to take some risks and spend a bit of money, time and effort to build a business, then the best time to start is *now*. The more you delay making a decision or buying a property, the more you delay your future rewards. You will never know everything. You need to know *enough* to get you started, but you will always be learning more about the business. You will always be improving and developing new ways and ideas for things to work better. Success does not arrive on day one – it is a more gradual and incremental process that develops over time. In fact, the more problems you meet and overcome, the more successful you will become. Challenges will make you grow.

Reading books, attending talks and going on courses are all great ways to boost your knowledge and help you feel you are 'fast-tracking' through the process. But taking the first step is the only way to really start the process. Find out as much as you can, research every angle, make yourself feel as knowledgeable as you possibly can and then *act*.

Action is what separates those who do and those who dream. And once you have started you will see a big change in your mind-set; you will no longer be an explorer, you will be an investor. This, in itself, will put you mentally in a different place. You will have proven to yourself: *you can do it*. And then when you know you can do it once, you will most likely look to do it again and again. Each time you will learn more, you will grow more, you will develop ways of doing things and thinking that you never thought possible. You will know what works for you, what makes you happy and what helps you to achieve your goals. And then you'll wonder why you didn't do it earlier. And you'll say: I wish I had started sooner . . . if only. So start today and act now.

Go For It!

Find a property you like and book an appointment to view it. Once you have seen it, you'll know if you want to do anything more about it.

Rule 7: What's the worst that could happen?

Expect the worst, hope for the best and
anything in between is not a surprise.

Almost anything you do in life comes with a set of risks. The key is in understanding the risks you are taking: what is it you are putting on the line to try to make something happen?

I have always lived by the philosophy: Expect the worst, hope for the best and anything in between is not a surprise. I'm not sure where I heard this or who it comes from, but it is a way of thinking that has served me well over the years.

So what is the worst that could happen if you invest in property?

At this stage, if it helps, you can get all catastrophic in your thinking. You can decide the worst that could happen is you will buy a property, the market will fall and you will lose 50 per cent of the value, the property won't let, and, when it finally does rent, it will go to a bad tenant who doesn't pay the rent and trashes it. Then, to top it all off, the tenant will burn the building down. In the meantime, you are struggling to make ends meet trying to pay the mortgage of the now-derelict property. There, how about that for a bad situation? Does that sound like the worst that could happen?

I reckon that sounds pretty disastrous – it would certainly put most investors off! But the key thing you need to ask yourself is: how likely is it that *all* of these events will happen – and *all* at once? And, if they did, how would you manage?

Well, let's unpack this for a moment to get to the bottom of the worst situation, as illustrated above. First, as long as you can afford to keep making your mortgage payments every month, the loss of value and no rent coming in doesn't actually affect your ownership of the property. Yes, it's a bugger you won't be getting the income; no, it's not good you will be losing rent every month; and yes, I agree everything you planned to happen hasn't – but you still have the property. Given time, the property will likely rise again in value and it will rent at some point for some money to somebody. Everybody has their price. Second, if a tenant trashes the place and then burns it down, you have insurance. Insurance may be a pain in the butt to pay for, but it's incredibly important. Insurance covers you for when stuff goes wrong and pays out for malicious damage and tenants burning down buildings. I know that, because I have been there and have had to make the claims!

When you analyse a worst-case scenario like this, you can plan. You can identify what you need to cover yourself for such a situation, should it ever happen. Having some money stashed away for times when the rent is not paid and making sure you have a decent insurance policy will mean you are well covered. So, if the worst ever does happen, you are ready in the best possible way.

Go For It!

Write down all your fears of the worst that could happen. Against each fear write down what you could do to prepare for that situation. Now you have a worst-case scenario and a plan of action.

Rule 8: Get real

High ambitions are great,
but actually what's more important
is to be realistic and get on and
achieve something.

Dreams. Aims. Ambitions. Always great to have them. Even better to meet them. But where to set them and where to start? High ambitions and dreams of empire building are great, but what's more important is to be realistic and get on and achieve *something*. Something is better than nothing. Setting your expectations too high can lead to disappointment and disillusionment. Moreover, it can also defeat the object and prevent you from starting in the first place. Aim too high and you won't even know how you are going to get there. So my advice for you is this: do something little by little.

Set realistic and achievable expectations. Start with buying one property, see how it goes and then progress from there. If you like the investment model and can see how it may work for you, then buy again. Then again. Then maybe some more. By focusing on the little-by-little approach, before you know it you will have amassed a portfolio that works for you. When you have a portfolio in place, you can decide what you want to do next. But the most important thing is to start. Don't overstretch yourself by thinking of all the high and mighty things you want to do before you've started. Just start.

Understand this is going to take *real* money. Forget anything you've heard that tries to tell you otherwise – property investment requires cold, hard cash. It costs money to buy property *and* it costs money to run and maintain your investment. Unless you are running some sort of secret button economy, you'll find money is the only way to pay for everything you need.

Be prepared to take on debt and for a long period of time. Unless you have a stash of cash ready to invest, you will most likely need to borrow money to finance your purchase. Prepare yourself for a lifetime of paying back other people's money and use borrowed money to make more of your own.

Don't be fooled into thinking this is passive income. Granted it's more passive than having to run an actual business that produces something, but property investment is still a business and will need work to ensure it gets off the ground and remains above water.

It takes time to understand investments. Not only does finding and looking after properties take time, but the market also takes time to rise for you to see any increase in capital appreciation. Cash flows also take time to feed through. Two hundred pounds profit may sound like a great bonus every month, but until the property is fully up and running you won't be seeing much of that extra money.

Being realistic with your expectations means you can set targets that you are more likely to achieve. And it's far better to achieve a target in the *real* world and make a difference to your *real* life than to dream of what might be and remain forever in your fantasy world.

Go For It!

Create momentum by doing at least one small action every day – for example, view a property, call a mortgage broker, check your savings, attend a property meet. Small actions snowball and create big things.

Rule 9: Learn to live on less and invest the rest

You get out what you put in.

Most people want to be rich. But most people are not prepared to do what it takes to get rich. Getting rich means changing your mind-set. It means putting in the hours, making the sacrifices and taking the risks for the rewards. Now, there are different levels of 'richness' and the riches you want may not require life-changing sacrifices, inordinate amounts of hard work and mammoth risk. But to achieve any form of wealth or success you are going to have to do *something*. You are going to have to give something if you expect to get something else in return. This is just a Rule of life.

You get out what you put in. The more you put in, the more you get out. But I find most people are not even prepared to give a little. They think they cannot live on less and they cannot work an extra hour or go without a bit of sleep. But if you want to achieve and get where you want to be, you will have to learn to do more. Unless you are prepared to change how you think about and live your life in order to achieve the bigger goal, you will stay where you are. I figure you don't want that – which is why you are reading this book.

Your mind-set needs to change now. You need to be willing to take that extra step, work that bit harder, and think and act differently. The saying goes: 'If you always do what you've always done, you'll always get what you've always got.' And the definition of madness is doing what you've always done and expecting different results! Different results don't just happen – they need to be produced. You need to think and act differently if you want to get something different to what you normally get. So what difference do you want? You need to put in the effort, money and time to build up to where you want to be. If you want to ditch the day job and become a full-time property investor, then you have got to put the necessary resources into it. It is not just going to happen overnight by magic.

So what do I expect you to put in? If you want to build a successful property business, I expect you to learn to live on less and invest the rest, at least in the beginning. You need to carefully manage your spending and commit to the long-term plan of investment. In the short term there will be sacrifices until you reach your goal – that's when you can enjoy the fruits of your labour. And there will be labour involved. Investing in property is not like buying a lottery ticket – you will not wake up one day to find you are rich. Successful investment requires a dream and a plan. The more you invest, the more you stand to gain. Time, effort, risk, money – the more you give, the more you get in potential rewards. So don't delay your future success, be prepared to do things differently and live your life to achieve your goals. Dreams can come true when you try hard enough.

Go For It!

Wake up thirty minutes earlier every day and spend time looking for investment opportunities. The more you look, the more you will learn, the more you will find.

Rule 10: Keep going

Keeping going is the single most important
factor in achieving success.

Determination. Resilience. Single-mindedness. You will need these in abundance. Property investment requires tenacity if you are to succeed. Deals do not magically appear in your lap. Money is not made automatically. You will need to work hard, focusing on your goal and what you are trying to achieve. People will try to scupper your plans: tenants will muck you about, buyers will mess around and vendors will wobble. Properties you thought were the deal of the century will turn out to be duds. The best-made plans will unravel. New challenges will arise and you will find yourself on what appears to be the route of a roller-coaster. Ups and downs, twists and turns will become a way of life. In time you will get used to the motion. And you will start to enjoy the ride. You will find it a thrill. But you have to get on-board and understand this way of thinking and live your life accordingly. Change is a fact of life – embrace it and use it to your advantage.

Brick walls will stop most people. They look at the wall and they say, 'This wall is too high, we can never make it over' or 'This wall is too thick, we can never make it through.' And for those people, they are right. The wall *is* too high and too thick. But for you, the wall is just another obstacle to overcome. It may well be a brick wall; however, *you* will find a way past it. You will take that wall down one brick at a time and you will make it through. Because you are not going to be stopped like most other people. You are going to succeed.

Keeping going is the single most important factor in achieving success. Most people start out on the journey with grand ambitions and ideas they want to achieve. They may be able to overcome the first few hurdles that beset them, but after time they get worn out, run down. They end up exhausted by the battle, the sheer constant trying. It's hard to keep going and say, 'Hit me again', and then get back up. Your energy levels drop, your desire to achieve wanes and your hope for the future dissipates. At this point, most people will give up. That leaves the route clear for those of us who are still trying. Bruised and battered you may be – but you are here, and you will remain here.

If you want to achieve, be prepared to achieve. The road is long and it will be bumpy. There will be detours, obstacles and all manner of things thrown in your way. There will be times when you run out of gas, when you lose your way on the sat nav and when you just don't know which way to go next. However, remember this: even if you have lost your way and don't know what to do, all you have to do is keep going. Eventually you will find yourself, and find the direction you want to head in. You will decide the way to go and you will carry on your journey as though it was all meant to be like this. Detours, distractions and losing direction are all part of the journey. Make them a part of the journey from the outset. Welcome them with open arms into your passenger seat. Turn to them and smile, and then just *keep going*.

Go For It!

Break down a BIG problem into little pieces and work out how to tackle each piece little by little. Problems can seem huge when left as a whole, but broken down they are just a collection of smaller tasks. Remember the saying: 'How do you eat an elephant? One bite at a time.'

Rule 11: Don't worry about what other people are doing

Just because other people are doing something, does not make it right for you.

In the world of property – where, I hasten to add, *everybody* is an expert, regardless of whether they own a property – it's easy to get side-tracked; to get distracted and listen to what other people are doing. New investment 'hot-spots' and innovative strategies for buying properties are always appearing on the market in ever more creative guises. We are awash with 'expert tips', 'inside knowledge', 'guru talks' and all manner of helpful information about what other people are doing. But note the phrase there: *other people.* Just because other people are doing something does not make it right for you. Other people can do what they want. You should focus on what *you* want to do.

The herd mentality is incredibly powerful – most likely because people don't want to miss out. People hate missing out; especially when it comes to making some money on property. Everybody wants to, and believes they can, make money in property. This means people look and listen more than they should: they are ready and waiting to be sold the dream.

Most of us want to take the path of least resistance. When we are offered an easy way to do something, we jump at the chance. Many armchair investment companies and portfolio-builders have flourished because they sell the ease and expertise of investment without you having to lift a finger – just transfer the cash. But really, ask yourself: do you actually want to do what other people are doing? Have you sat down and thought about what you *want* to be doing?

Property is a personal choice and what you hope to get out of it should be dictated by your personal objectives. Your objectives will be different to mine. Yes, we can agree we both want to make some money out of this, but how we make and take that money will differ according to what we want to achieve and by when.

The grass always looks greener on the other side. Other people always seem to be doing better stuff, more interesting stuff, stuff that will make more money. Or so it appears. What somebody says may be very different to what it actually is. And anyway, just because everybody else is doing it doesn't make it right. So, while it's good to listen and learn from what other people are doing, don't be tempted to rush off and automatically copy them. Take time to do your own research and think about your objectives. Don't be afraid to be different – if it makes sense to you and you believe your plan can work, go for it! This is your property investment career – not other people's – so make sure it stays that way.

Go For It!

Meet with a friend and discuss your retirement plans. How much do you have in common? How different are your plans to theirs?

Rule 12: Your opinion matters

*You are the only person who
actually matters.*

Starting out in property investment can feel like a big deal – and it *is* a big deal. For that reason, it's understandable why so many people seek out the advice of experts. It can be a great source of inspiration and wisdom to learn from those who have been there and done it. However, as with most things in life, many people have different opinions. And when it comes to property investment, most people will proffer an opinion, whether they are an expert or not!

Knowing who to listen to and what advice to take can be incredibly difficult when there are so many varying points of view and ways of doing things. However, the key person who should never be overlooked or not listened to is *you*. You are the only person who actually matters; it is you who will be investing in property and you who will be taking the risk. Not that bloke down the pub, nor your friend from next door – not even the expert whose course you attended. You will be the owner of the property and therefore it is you who should be listened to. Because, like it or not, it will be down to you to make this a success – or it will be you for the chopping block when it fails. Either way, the success or failure of this investment is down to you.

I know that sounds scary – which is why you wanted

advice, and why you sought guidance. But the key thing you have to understand is how you feel. You are the only one who knows how comfortable you feel with the risks you may have to take. You are the one who knows how well you will be able to sleep at night knowing you owe money on a mortgage. It is you who knows your finances inside out, and how well you will be able to deal with a non-paying tenant, or a property that does not sell. You need to listen to yourself. Anybody and everybody can give you a gazillion different ideas and tactics as to how to deal with these scenarios – but ultimately it will be down to you to enact them. And it is only you who knows how well you will be able to perform when the time comes.

So at this juncture let me tell you that, regardless of what I or anybody else says, it is only *your* opinion that matters. That may seem a strange thing for me to say in the context of this book, but it is only *you* who can take action and do what you believe is right for you. Other people may have their own ideas – that's fine, and each may work for them – but you must always remember that what is right for somebody else does not make it right for you. Never ever belittle yourself because you feel you don't know enough, or don't have enough. Your opinion on how to take your investment forwards is what is important. And really that's all that matters.

Go For It!

Start an e-petition for a cause you care about.

Rule 13: Grow a pair . . .

Successful property investment
requires courage.

Property investment takes balls. It doesn't matter what anybody says, or how easy they make it look; buying a property to make money involves taking risks. And it entails large sums of money. You won't always get it right, you won't always know what you are doing, and a lot of the time you will be exposed to market trends and macro factors that are way out of your control. And so when you get into the business of property investment you need to have courage. But for those of you who are brave enough, the rewards can be magnificent. Remember the saying: Fortune favours the brave.

Getting out of your comfort zone is *uncomfortable*. It is challenging, it is different, it is not what you are used to. Your comfort zone is *comfortable* and you like it like that. But stepping out of your comfort zone makes you feel good. Expanding on your knowledge and your capabilities makes you grow as a person. How much can you really grow when you are not challenged? Challenge makes us stronger. It makes us more capable, and, while at the time it may not seem like it, in the end it makes us more confident. And confidence breeds courage.

Successful property investment requires courage. You may have a plan and know what you want, but that is not to say your plan will always happen. Plans can and do change. What you thought you were going to do may not, in the end, be what happens. It may not be of your making, it may be down to the market changing or it may be due to a variety of other factors. And this is the risk of property investment, which requires courage. It should not be undertaken lightly. But nor should it be built up into some unattainable and difficult dream.

You need to be realistic. You need to understand that property doesn't always make money and property isn't always fun. There are going to be tough times and difficult periods ahead. You have to be prepared to grow as a person and deal with the stuff that will happen – because stuff *will* happen. Investing in property is not the same as saving your money in the bank. There are consequences to your investment and matters that you will have to deal with. There will be some hard decisions to make, maybe even some hardship you will suffer. It will not all be easy. And at times you will wonder why you made your life so hard.

It is during these times that you will really need to grow a pair. Making money is not easy. In fact, it is very hard. But doing nothing is also a risk. Not making a decision is risky. The world is always moving, and – whether we like it or not – our world will get changed for us. Make change an active choice and get used to being comfortable with uncomfortable.

Go For It!

Do something new outside your comfort zone and challenge yourself. You can make it as easy or hard as you want; for example, go to the pub on your own, sign up for a karaoke night – or how about a bungee jump?

Rule 14: Think like the boss

The buck stops with you.

Unless you are already running your own business, this is possibly one of the hardest things to get your head around. Thinking like the boss means the buck stops with you. That means whatever happens, even if it was somebody else's fault or someone else's responsibility, you take the fall. I know it sounds unfair – it is – but this is part of being the boss. And when you are the boss, everything is down to you.

To be the boss you need broad shoulders. And it helps if you remember to count to ten. Often. People will let you down, lie and cheat, but that is all part of the magic of working with other people. As the boss, your job is to manage this. There is no point in thinking or trying to do everything yourself. Yes, many things can be done by you, I'm sure; however, there will come a point when you'll need to delegate. The art of successful delegation will then make you somebody's boss. That means you need to give clear instructions.

The best way to be a more successful boss is to understand from the start: *you are the boss*. How things pan out and any future success or failure will be down to you. Now that you know that and it's clear, I think you may start thinking differently about a project. That plumber you met down the pub and who seemed cheap – is he really the best option for you to get the job done? Or how about that letting agent with the special offer management fee or the estate agent with a fee-free sale – what service level will they actually provide for nothing? You need to think like the boss and ask yourself: am I really making the best decisions that will lead to the best outcomes? Am I really doing the most I can, or am I trying to dodge responsibility and thinking it's down to somebody else?

Being the boss means taking responsibility for the whole project, not just the management part. Your name is on the land registry deeds and the ownership of the property is yours. To really make a success of a project you're going to have to understand that it's your neck on the line. Just think of it like a railway line and you'll get the gist of how important this is.

Being the boss can feel uncomfortable at the start, so, if it helps, take a step outside of yourself and pretend to be somebody who's used to doing the job. Pretend you are capable, confident and competent: *you are the boss*. This tactic, otherwise known as 'fake it until you make it', can work miracles. And this strategy will get you through until you really do start thinking and acting like the boss!

Go For It!

Delegate a task to somebody (it can be any task, not necessarily one that's property related). Give clear instructions, including what needs to be done, by when and what the expected outcome is. Manage the process and learn from what worked and what didn't work. Then delegate another task.

Rule 15: Don't be shark bait

The property dream industry is not the same as the property industry.

Desperation stinks. You can smell it a mile off. And it attracts the wrong sort of people. These are the sorts of people who claim they are going to help you (and it may initially seem they can do so), but who actually *harm* you. Not physically (not that I've heard of), but they will *financially* harm you. They will present themselves as experts who can teach you, train you and educate you in the ways of how to get rich and make a mint from property. They will claim to have access to exclusive deals and a network of people in the know. And on the face of it, they may seem genuine. They may appear very successful and have all the trappings of wealth and the fancy lifestyle you aspire to. Some may even take on the status of 'guru'.

And when someone is presented as a 'guru', it can seem hard to question them, treacherous even to question their abilities and claims. But do it. Question now. Before you do anything else: question the expert. Do not be afraid to dig deep into their lives, to ask them: why are you teaching me to get rich? What's in it for you? Because nobody, I repeat nobody, does something for nothing; especially if that person is supposedly teaching you to get rich.

Making money from property is a widely held dream, and this dream is something many people have created into a side-industry of its own. Let's call it the 'property dream industry'. It co-exists alongside the property industry, but it is not one and the same. That is the difference you need to be aware of: the property dream industry is *not* the same as the property industry. Being trained in how to buy property is different to actually buying property. For some, learning how you do something is enough, and they don't feel the need to actually then do it. But it is critical you are aware of the difference and don't fool yourself into thinking you are doing, when you are only learning about doing.

When you want to do something so badly – when you are prepared to go to any lengths in order to get started – attending a course or going for training can seem a small price to pay in return for achieving your dream. But just be sure you *will* be achieving your dream, rather than becoming a part of the dream industry and selling your dream to achieve somebody else's.

My advice to you: dream it; do it.

Go For It!

Conduct research on a mentor. Search the internet for reviews of any experts.

Rule 16: Have selective hearing

'Never take advice from someone you wouldn't pay or swap places with.'

My mother used to always say to me: 'You only hear what you want to hear.' She still says it to this day, calling it my 'selective hearing switch'. While I'm sure she had a different meaning behind her words, the 'selective hearing switch' is actually a fantastic skill to have in property investment. Once you get into the business, you will find lots of people tell you lots of things. Some of it will be true, parts will be useful and the rest will be downright lies. Of course, understanding the difference is where success lies.

Understanding the difference can be very difficult in the beginning when there are so many people to listen to and so much knowledge to take on board. However, the essence of 'selective hearing' is about knowing *when* to listen and *who* to listen to. That may sound a tall order when you are just starting out, but a friend of mine, who is a very successful property investor, sums it up nicely in the following: 'Never take advice from someone you wouldn't pay or swap places with.' Those are fantastic words of wisdom for understanding when to use your 'selective hearing switch'. If you would not be prepared to pay for the advice, nor want to swap places with the person giving it, then is that *really* right for you?

With so many sources of advice on offer, it is critical you have some sort of criteria for selecting those people whom you choose to listen to and filtering through the advice they are giving. Much of this will depend upon where you are and where you hope to be on your investment journey. I would advise you to pick people whom you aspire to be like and whom you genuinely like and believe in. Many investors have different business models and it is important you listen to those people who fit with your attitude to life and your style of investing. High risk, high reward is not for everyone, just as buying-to-let or hands-on property development is not for others. The key is in understanding what you want and finding people who fit what you are looking for.

Don't be afraid to take a pic 'n' mix approach to investment knowledge. You can select advice from here, you can get guidance from there and you can admire somebody from elsewhere. All of these sources are to be used and exploited. There are no right or wrong ways. The aim and the eventual outcome is what matters – you need to feel inspired and ready to be the best property investor you can be.

Go For It!

Learn when to tune in and when to tune out. Turn off listening to or reading bad news stories and use that time to educate yourself positively, such as through watching cultural or historical programmes or downloading business podcasts.

Rule 17: Be a winning negotiator

Don't make promises you can't deliver on.

Negotiation is more of an art form than a science. It is a skill you need to learn and develop in double-quick time if you are to get on. Negotiation is involved at every level in property investment, from trying to find a property to buy, to renting it out and making a sale. You'll need to deal with people and, be they vendors, agents, solicitors, surveyors, tenants or buyers, it all involves negotiation. The only way you can become a winning negotiator is to practise – and that means, start doing it.

People claim lots of different tricks work for them, from waxing lyrical about neuro-linguistic programming (NLP) to strategising like a chess grandmaster. Personally, I think this is all a bit over the top. You need to evaluate what a deal is worth to you and work out the important bits and not-so-important bits you can barter on. And it's important to always be nice if you want to win. People like nice people – and while nice may sound a bit pedestrian you'd be surprised how many people are *not* nice – and niceness costs nothing. So start with being nice. Then progress to being smart. And when I say smart, I don't mean 'shove it in their face how clever and amazing you are'; just quietly show you know what you are talking about. You don't have to boast and brag, but you do need to display your knowledge – just enough so that anyone you deal with knows you know what you are talking about.

Be confident and reassuring. Nobody likes to be messed about. Don't make promises you can't deliver on. If you're not a cash buyer, don't say you are. Agents will ask for proof and unless you can show proof of funds you will look like a fool and lose all credibility. Be ready to move, if you say you are ready to move. Have your dream team of professionals lined up (solicitors, surveyors, brokers, etc.) and set to go. This will make you more confident and able to act with authority when it comes down to the nitty-gritty.

Don't get upset. Emotions need to be kept in check when negotiating. Tact and diplomacy are key. Getting highly strung can lead to saying and doing things you may regret later. You don't always have to play 'poker face' and it is OK to be keen, but don't be desperate. Try not to make your first offer your last move and leave a little 'wiggle' room to work with. When you get to your 'best and final' offer, make that plain. People need to know when a limit has been reached. You can leave your offer on the table. But when your limit has been reached, declare it and walk away to find another deal.

Always look to create a win-win situation – successful negotiation means you have both won. You want to pay as little as you can, but the vendor wants as much as they can get. Don't be afraid to offer so low you feel a little 'red faced', but don't go so low that you feel ashamed. Making an offer too low will most likely cause annoyance and upset, which is difficult to come back from. Find out any information that may be useful in your negotiation – such as that the vendor is looking for a quick sale – and then leverage that into your sales pitch. Successful negotiation means that every party needs to feel like a winner. The best and easiest way to succeed is by treating others the way you want to be treated. Being nice is a far-too-often-overlooked trait. Try it – you'll be surprised by just how far it gets you.

Go For It!

Call one of your service providers such as your telephone or insurance company. Try to negotiate a better deal than your current one. Remember, it may not always be about paying less, but about getting value for money.

Rule 18: Keep a trust bank account

Trust is the currency of modern life.

Trust is a precious commodity. It underlies nearly all of our transactions in life. Some may even argue trust is more precious than money. It is the backbone of life in society. Without trust our entire system would break down. That's just how important trust is: it is the currency of modern life. Without trust, the world would be an incredibly difficult, if not impossible, place in which to operate. And, given its importance, it's quite surprising how taken for granted this concept is. Until trust is broken – then you understand how integral it is to life.

Trust is not a given. There are no automatic trust machines. It must be earned. Like money, trust builds over time. The easiest way to think about trust is as a bank account: a giant trust bank account. Every time somebody does something they said they were going to do, they earn a credit. It's as though they are depositing into your trust bank account. Over time these credits and deposits build up and earn a 'trust balance'. But every time somebody doesn't do what they were meant to, they deduct from the trust account: they make a withdrawal from the 'trust balance'.

Trust is integral to successful property investment and you should keep a careful eye on your trust bank account.

Accounts with people should not be allowed to go too far into the red. Limits should be imposed and deadlines adhered to. You should think of your role as akin to a bank manager and your job is to ensure that people remain in credit rather than fall into debt. Because too much debt is a bad thing, and too much mistrust will mean you can no longer operate effectively.

Many times when people make a withdrawal, it's not through any fault of their own – they may intend something to happen but, for whatever reason, it doesn't. Tenants don't move in, buyers don't buy or people don't pay as and when they should. This can cause major trauma and can result in your losing trust in people. The trust balance goes into the red, and you feel as though you are overdrawn. You are forced to trust people who you no longer feel you can trust. This is an uncomfortable situation.

Trust needs to be built and it takes time. But to speed up the process (and thereby understand earlier on if someone is trustworthy) you can set 'trust targets'. For example, requesting a call back from an estate agent at a set time and date. If they manage it, they have earned a modicum of trust: they have done what they said they would do. If they don't, they have already started to withdraw trust from the account. And there is only so much that can be withdrawn from an account before you pull the plug.

Never be afraid to cut your losses, as sometimes it is the only way back into credit. And don't forget that debt is toxic and can spread quicker than you realise. Be careful not to allow mistrust to seep into other areas of your life. Your trust bank balance is much more important than you realise and should never be taken for granted.

Go For It!

Set a 'trust target' with an agent. Call for details about a property and request a call back.

Rule 19: You need to be able to sleep at night

Operating without a safety net is
akin to financial suicide.

Risk is all around us. But when you start investing in property, especially buying property to rent, you increase your exposure to risk. Not only will you be juggling loan repayments and repair bills while keeping an eye on interest rates and rents that are due in, but you will also be walking the tightrope of ever-changing legislation and regulation in the housing market. Add to that, lenders changing their terms and conditions, tenants not behaving and the property market not performing as it should, and you have a healthy dose of risk that will substantially increase your heart rate.

Anybody who thinks investing in property is risk-free is delusional. There are risks associated with any form of investment, and property is no different. Of course, different properties have different risk profiles and this is something you should look into carefully before buying. Risk can take many forms but, in essence, much of it boils down to financial risk. Tenants not paying the rent, mortgage rates increasing, values falling, boilers breaking, and a multitude of other stuff that can and does happen is actually all about money.

Most risk in property investment can be mitigated by having access to money. Regardless of what the issue is, it can usually be sorted by *paying* for it to be sorted, whether it is a boiler that needs replacing or a property that has fallen in value. In the former, money will be required to pay for the repair bill; in the latter, money will be required to tide you over until the market recovers or for you to pay down the debt so that you can sell. Having access to money sorts and solves most property issues.

This is why it is essential you have a financial buffer when you invest in property. Operating without a safety net is akin to financial suicide. The risks you are exposing yourself to are massive and will cause many sleepless nights. The only way to overcome the risks of property investment are by planning for them and creating a buffer so that when some of these risks materialise (and they will at some point) you are ready and prepared. That way, you do not risk losing your entire investment – because *that* is the greatest risk of all.

So get yourself ready to be able to sleep at night. Create a financial duvet to cushion you and protect your investments from the problems that may arise. That way you will be able to sleep soundly knowing your investments are safe.

Go For It!

If you do not have a financial buffer, create one now, or at least start saving towards it. You should always have, in a separate bank account, the equivalent of at least six months' rent for a property.

Rule 20: Do what others are not prepared to do

Real money is made from doing the stuff most other people don't want to do.

Most investors are lazy. They want to buy a property, have it shoot up in value and then sell it for a ton of money. They want easy tenants who look after the property like a show home and always pay the rent on time. They want buyers who will pay the price they decide and wire the money yesterday. They want deals that fall into their lap at bargain prices and with minimal work to do. That's fine and good luck to them. That will account for a very small percentage of the market that is trouble-free and massively in demand. The rest of the market, also known as the *real world*, is where *real* money is made. Real money is made from doing the stuff most other people don't want to do.

Most people don't want to do too much or put too much effort in, which means there's plenty out there for you to be getting on with. It might involve taking more risks, such as gaining planning permission or undertaking a development project. It may be about dealing with a more difficult property that has issues, or managing tenants at a different end of the market. It may even involve sourcing your properties using alternative proactive methods such as leafleting key areas. Whatever way you choose, there is money to be made in areas where people don't want to do anything – or where they can't see what could be done. Spotting an opportunity and working in an area of the market where most other people don't want to work can be a golden opportunity that can give you the chance to find and own your niche – and make your own riches.

So how do you go about doing this? Well, what you're *not* going to do is what most other people do. You are going to take the route *off* the mainstream and find a specialised area you can work in and that can work for you. It doesn't matter what bit of the market you choose as long as you like it, can see potential and believe it will make money. It really is that simple.

For me, buying property at auction has been my specialist area for many years, but it is just one of many. Shared properties are great cash cows, and large buildings with conversion potential to smaller units can offer additional capital uplift. The benefit sector, a section of the tenant population shunned by so many investors, can offer high rewards if you select and manage your customers well. Commercial properties, often overlooked by many small investors, can offer strong income yields and additional opportunities for mixed-use future residential potential. Serviced accommodation, land banking, ex-council houses, non-standard construction and tower block homes all offer different entry points and rewards to investors.

There is no *one* way or *right* way to make money – there are so many opportunities available to you, you just have to choose your pitch and work it!

Go For It!

Actively seek out alternative markets and other ways of doing things. Look for niche areas where you can specialise and that have the potential for profit. Learn more about them with a view to future investment.

Rule 21: Get a GSOH

Those who can laugh are best
equipped to make it through.

I know it may sound like some sort of lonely hearts ad – 'Needs to have GSOH' (Good Sense of Humour) – but I'm telling you, you have to find the funny side if you're going to survive. People will do the strangest of things and your best armour against this will be to laugh. Often. Now, what I don't mean is to laugh in someone's face, but it helps if you can find the amusement factor from a crap situation. Stuff is going to happen. Some of it will make you incredibly angry, some of it will make you sad, some of it will be enough to make you want to hide under the duvet and never come out. When you get into property investment, you are welcoming the potential for a lot more challenging stuff in your life. And you have to accept and expect this. Life is about to get a whole lot more interesting, so it's wise to smile about the choices you have made and the situations you may find yourself in.

You know the saying: 'You make your bed, you lie in it.' This is kind of how it is. You have chosen the path of property investment. You have chosen to make your life, shall we say, more *challenging*. But you have chosen this path because you are focusing on the bigger goal and the better life you want for yourself. Your bed today may not be how you want it made, but at least you are on your way to making it how you want it to be in the future.

Not everything that happens will be fun. Not every part of investing in property will be a laugh a minute. Some of the time it will be draining: financially, emotionally and physically. That is why you need to keep things light. You need to remember the bright side of life and, wherever possible, to replace anger with amusement. Things are sometimes going to be tough. This is not a television show – the only happy ending is of your own making.

Those who can laugh are best equipped to make it through. Being upset gets you down and wastes energy; having a laugh brings you up and energises you. Yes, there will be times when laughter is inappropriate, when you are in the frying pan and the oil is burning badly. But do you want to sizzle or do you want to burn?

It's all about mind-set; and coping mechanisms. It's about creating strategies to get you through when the chips are down and when you are seriously burning. Making light of things will enable you to see the light. You will often wonder how long the tunnel is going to go on for and if there is even a light at the end of it. But this is when you need to create your own light. You need to find the path for you, and that means being able to smile at what you've got yourself into, the life you have chosen, and know that someday you will be able to look back and laugh – so you may as well try to do it now.

Go For It!

Take a moment to sit or stand. Imagine your stomach smiling a big cheesy grin. Notice how your face can't help but smile when you imagine your stomach smiling. Smile ☺.

Rule 22: Get out of your shell

You can never know too many people.

Being a successful property investor means talking to a lot of people, a lot of the time. If you don't like talking, you'd better start getting to like it now, because you're going to be talking a lot! Whether you're buying to sell, buying to rent or wanting to sell or rent your property, you're going to have to involve a number of different people in the process. And the process is easier if you know more people. Remember: you can never know too many people.

Try to make the most of every connection, and promise yourself that you will attempt to meet more people in the property industry. Having a wide network of such people will make your life easier, and it will benefit your business enormously. It may seem difficult to begin with, but the more you do it the easier it will get, until it becomes second nature to ask for business cards and people's contact details.

In these days of social media and internet forums, building a property network is a whole lot easier than you think. The key is to get started.

So let's get you started.

- **Events:** Lots of property networking events take place all over the country. Most offer a speaker on a topical subject with opportunities to network. There is usually a nominal fee payable for attendance. Meetup.com is a great resource for locating property groups in your area. The calibre of events can vary so do some research before you sign up. At first, talking to strangers can be intimidating, but remember you are also a stranger to them. People attend these events because they want to meet and talk with other people – as do you. Smile at everyone and don't be afraid to start the ball rolling. After all, how hard is it to say, 'Hi, how are you?'

- **Twitter:** Get yourself an account and start following people in property. There are loads you might choose, from journalists and estate agents to solicitors and property publications. Read tweets, post stuff, engage in conversations, and before you know it you will start to gain your own following. Within weeks you will have a whole new network of property people.

- **Facebook/LinkedIn/Google+:** I'm sure you probably already use these sites to catch up with your friends and colleagues, but in addition to letting you chat and post updates they offer you great opportunities to join groups and meet like-minded people. Search for property groups and join those you feel look interesting. Before long you will receive updates on property news from the group and have the opportunity to join in conversations. Share interesting content you have found (if you join Twitter and follow property people, you'll have plenty) and make a point of getting involved.

- **Internet forums:** There are a huge number of property forums freely available on the internet. These sites can be a fantastic resource and a great way to start meeting other people in property. Joining in the conversation is key if you want to start building relationships. Even if you don't feel able to add expertise in the beginning, just saying, 'Thanks for sharing' to a poster shows you are there. Many internet forums have a friendly, community feel to them and embrace new members with open arms.

Go For It!

Take a few minutes to register for a free account; find an event, group, forum; and join in! Make your presence known by saying or sharing something.

Rule 23: Don't over-share online

*Your conversations leave a global
online footprint for all and
sundry to see and search.*

Social media has become a part of everyday life. Using your phone to log on to Facebook or Twitter for status updates is now more normal than using it for actual telephone calls. Connections can be made with the click of a button and networking has taken on a whole new level. The social media world encourages sharing; *sharing is caring*. We 'Like', 'retweet', '+1', 'pin' and comment to our heart's content. But with all this social sharing going on, there is a temptation to perhaps 'over-share'. Details of our lives, inner thoughts and intimate actions become announced to the world. And, in this new social world, the issue is: you do not know who is listening or watching.

Privacy rules and settings are a minefield. Social media sites continually change their terms and conditions and the small print is bamboozling. The best rule of thumb is not to say anything you don't want the rest of the world to know. That may sound extreme, but you'd be surprised how many friends of friends can connect you to a gazillion different strangers, whom you neither know nor mean to share your life with.

Having an online presence is a great way to boost your

profile and connect with people, but it is important to ensure you manage your online persona and reputation. Your social media profile doesn't just exist on the internet; online is increasingly converging with off-line. But, unlike people in the real world, search engines never forget what you post. That is why you need to be careful what you say – and also *how* you say it. Your conversations leave a global online footprint for all and sundry to see and search.

Increasingly, the ever-watchful eye of Big Brother is upon us – and via social media we have invited him in to share the minutiae of our lives. But this invitation is no longer just personal and private to our network – more and more our private photos and comments are being used in the public arena. People have found themselves out of a job or out of a relationship due to posting inappropriate photos or comments. Private is the new public.

You may think this doesn't affect you, but you'd be surprised at the number of people who Google other people before they meet them or make key decisions. Your off-hand comments to your best friend about spending all your money, may be viewed in an entirely different light by a bank from which you were hoping to obtain a loan. That's the issue with the internet: anything and everything you say may be found and interpreted in ways you never imagined, and sometimes used against you. This is why the utmost care should be taken with what you say online: because you never know when it may become real in the off-line world.

Go For It!

Review what you have posted on social media sites and think about what you are projecting to the rest of the world. Delete any inappropriate photos and/or posts.

Rule 24: Buy time, not stuff (a.k.a. spend less, invest the rest!)

Time is all we have to make the most of our lives.

Time is all we have. Time is unreplenishable. You cannot stock up on time. You cannot buy it back. Once your time's up; your time's up. Each and every one of us, no matter who we are, only has twenty-four hours in the day. But it's how we use that time that defines and divides us. Time is what divides the rich from the poor. The rich have time to do things: they live; the poor are busy trying to make ends meet: they survive. And yet so many of us choose to make ourselves poor because of the choices we make. We don't realise, until it's too late, that time is all we have to make the most of our lives.

Time poverty is a very real phenomenon, but it is one that many of us have created for ourselves. The consumerism that is rife in our society is testament to that. If we valued our time more, we wouldn't be awash with so much *stuff* in our lives. From fancy cars to big houses, exotic holidays and the latest must-haves, all this stuff we have and covet is paid for in our time. You sell your time to your employer in exchange for money. How you spend that money shows how you value your time. That dress you really had to have, that big TV you really wanted, the Sky subscription, the iPhone – you sold your time to obtain that stuff.

But how about living life a different way? How about valuing you and your time more, and making time more important than money? With more time in your life, you'd have the time to write that book, start that company or develop that idea. Time would give you the freedom to pursue the things you've always dreamt of doing. And most likely those things would *make* you money, unlike the stuff you spend your time on now, which *takes* your money. How you spend your money now and every purchase you make is a deduction from your present and future life – from time you could have had. Just imagine that. Look around you now and calculate how much of your time you have spent on accumulating things. How many hours did you work to buy your TV, your laptop or your car? How much better could that money and time have been spent?

Time is the only currency that matters. Time is valuable. It is a limited resource. You should value and cherish your time. Go without stuff and you'll be amazed at how little you need. The less you need, the less you will have to sell your time in exchange for money, and the more time you will have. Think about your choices more. Think about what you are exchanging your life for and ask yourself: 'How do I want to spend my time?' Focus on buying less to get more. Use your money to buy time, not stuff. Investing in property is about investing in you and your future – so spend less and invest the rest!

Go For It!

Work out how much you earn net per hour and then calculate the value of the items you are spending your money and time on. Is buying that new TV really worth your exchanging *X* hours of your life?

Rule 25: Know when enough is enough

Knowing when you have enough gives you the freedom to live the life you want to live.

People often get het up about the number of properties they want to own, be it five, ten, twenty, fifty or even over a hundred. I remember talking to somebody once who wanted to own fifty-two properties. Their reasoning being: they wanted a property for every week of the year! Targets are great. Goals should be set. Plans should be made. However, when planning on investing in property, it is important you make the right plans and understand how you are judging your outcomes. Very rarely does the number of properties you own equate to the amount of success or money you will reap in the end. A more useful barometer, and much more meaningful result, is how much money you have made, or are set to make, from investing.

For some people, making an extra £200 per month would enable them to survive; others would not be satisfied unless there were an extra two zeros on the end of that. Again others aren't fussed about extra income every month, but focus on a big pay cheque at the end of a refurbishment project. Whatever sort of person you are, and whatever your goals, it is important to know when *enough is enough*. 'What?' I hear you cry. 'How can enough ever be enough?' In reply I would have to answer: 'We should all know when we have enough.'

The reasoning behind this Rule is that, no matter what you do, you will most likely feel you *never* have enough. Regardless of what you *do* have, somebody will always have more. And that can feel tough. It can feel hard to accept that somebody has X more money, or a better car than you. But rather than running yourself ragged trying to get more than them, it's important to stay focused on what you *do* have and when you have *enough* – it doesn't actually matter then what other people have.

Understanding when enough is enough brings peace, contentment, and an ability to move on and become a different person. No longer part of the rat race, you will be free to be who you want to be and do what you want to do. The sense and understanding that comes from knowing when you have enough will give you a freedom that is very difficult to buy, no matter how many investments you make. Racing against yourself and other people is a very hard contest to win, and there will come a time when you have to ask yourself: 'Do I still want to compete?'

Knowing when you have enough gives you the freedom to live the life you want to live. Property investment is so much more than just buying a bunch of bricks and mortar: it is an investment in you and in your life plan. So now you have your plan and your properties, go off and live your life.

Go For It!

Find a box of crayons, like those you used to draw with when you were a child. Open the box and smell them. Close your eyes and drink in the memories of being a child again, happily colouring in pictures with your crayons. Remember and enjoy the moment of freedom. Tastes good, doesn't it?

PART TWO: PROPERTY RULES

Properties can be liabilities as well as assets. This means you need to know how to look for properties that have potential, and how to avoid properties that can become money pits. Property Rules are the criteria you need to put in place to understand and define the type of investments you want to make. There are millions of properties to choose from and it is essential you have a way of deciding which of them fit with your objectives and future goals. Every investor has their own way of choosing the properties they invest in and why, and it's important you buy the right property for you. Properties come in all shapes and sizes and there is no 'one-size-fits-all'.

So take the time to work on what properties you want to invest in, your Property Rules, and let's get you started on finding the right sort of properties for you.

Rule 26: Buying is just the beginning

Properties not only cost a massive amount to buy, they cost a lot of money to run.

Investing in property does not instantly make you money. In fact, once you own a property, you will start to learn just how *expensive* property investment can be! Properties not only cost a massive amount to buy, they also cost a lot of money to run. The running costs of long-term investments, plus the front-heavy capital nature of the business, are often overlooked by many novices in the early stages.

Property investment is not just a case of 'buy a property and sit and wait until the asset is worth double what you paid'. Although that can happen, in the meantime the property needs to be looked after and maintained if it is to provide you with an income. This 'looking after' aspect, and the amount of money required for the upkeep, is something many investors tend to conveniently forget when doing their initial sums. However, this maintenance is a key aspect of ensuring your investment retains both its capital value and income streams, and produces the rental yields you anticipated.

Every property has different maintenance requirements depending upon the type, age and build; whether any upgrade works have been done; and the type of tenant who will be in occupation. However, while there are different levels of wear and tear, a good rule of thumb is to allow at least 10–15 per cent of the monthly rental for ongoing maintenance. This percentage of the rent should be hived off every month via a standing order and saved in a separate bank account. This separation of the maintenance monies will ensure that when bills come in (and they will) you have funds set aside to pay them.

Undertaking routine maintenance when issues arise is not only a key part of good customer service – it is also a preventative measure to avoid future major expense. Routine maintenance tasks can quickly turn into much larger issues if they are left or ignored, and can land you with a much more expensive repair bill. Take, for example, a small water leak. It may not seem much of an issue in the beginning. However, if it is not put right it can start to do untold damage – much of which you may not see before the real damage becomes apparent. A small leak can trickle away unnoticed for years, seeping into floorboards and rotting joists. It may only be when you see staining on the ceiling or floor that you start to take notice. However, by that point the small leak is likely to have caused major damage to the internal fabric of the building and you could end up with a repair bill in the thousands rather than the small amount it would have cost you to fix the leak in the first place.

Property investment is not a one-hit wonder – it requires a continual drip-feed of funds if your investment is to provide you with an income and grow in capital value. Maintaining your investment is key to maintaining your future wealth.

Go For It!

Calculate what 10–15 per cent of your predicted monthly rental amount would be, and allow this for routine maintenance.

Rule 27: You're not buying for you

Liking a property you purchase is different to buying a property you like.

Property is an emotional purchase and, even when investing, it is difficult not to get caught up. Trying to rid yourself of the emotional aspect is pointless – people buy and rent properties according to how they make them feel. It's better and easier to embrace the emotional, 'touchy-feely' part of the investment – but understand it for what it is: how the property makes you feel. This understanding of your emotional response to a property will enable you to separate your feelings from the investment objectives. Emotions can cloud decisions and so it is best to be aware of how you are affected and how your objectivity may in fact be subjective!

Properties bought for investment need to be just that: bought for investment. Liking a property you purchase is different to buying a property you like. Properties you like are those that you might want to move into or could envisage yourself living in – they are not likely to be the best investment decisions. What *you* like is not necessarily what someone else likes. Remember, when you are buying an investment property, you are buying for someone else – this objective must always be kept front of mind. Often people claim you should invest in a property that you would live in yourself, but there is a fundamental difference between buying a property that you want to live in yourself and buying an investment property for someone else to live in. One is your home, the other is somebody else's home. Trying to marry up these two perspectives can create compromises that may affect your investment decisions.

Property bought for investment must meet a different set of criteria to property bought for you to live in. Investment purchases must be thoroughly researched and tested with the target market they are aimed at. Audience groups have very different requirements and it is critical you make your investment property as attractive as you can to the target market. Trying to be all things to all people will mean the property lacks 'punch' and is unlikely to stand out from the crowd. Properties have their own unique personalities and each should be worked with to ensure it fits well with your intended audience. By understanding what your target market is looking for, you will be able to design and develop a property that suits their needs and wants. This will connect and resonate far more strongly on both the emotional and functional level and will lead to increased investment success.

Go For It!

Get into the mind-set of your target audience. Think about how they would search for the properties they want to live in. Make a list of the things they would be looking for such as number of bedrooms, proximity to transport connections, local schools, etc.

Rule 28: You have to kiss a lot of frogs

It is better to secure the right investment
from the start than to invest quickly.

I read somewhere that most investors will view one hundred properties before seeing two they like. This means that, out of the properties you will see, you will most likely only want to buy one in fifty. That is a pretty low rate, but in my experience it probably sounds about right. In the beginning, it can be frustrating trying to find the right investment, but it is important to enjoy the journey rather than rush a purchase. You are not in a race. Yes, you want to get started – but it is better to secure the right investment from the start than to invest quickly – one right one is far better than five wrong ones!

Starting to view property as an investment is a whole new ball game to looking at property you are thinking of living in yourself. For one thing, you are *not* going to live there. That is a major hurdle that you need to get over. No matter how great the property is, or how much you like the area, this purchase is *not* for you: it is for somebody else. It is your target market – your end customers – who will be living there and so it is important to bear in mind that person, not you.

Buying with someone else in mind takes a lot of courage

and confidence. You want to be sure you are investing in the right property for your audience. However, it is a skill that, with research and time, *can* be learned and can be honed really rather well. You may even find, after a while, that it's easier to know what to buy for your customers than it is for yourself! The skill to successful property investment is in knowing what other people want and what they are looking for. Thorough and ongoing research is the key to getting this right.

Although an investment property is not going to be your home, it is vital you feel comfortable with it. This is your investment and it's likely you're going to be carrying a lot of debt on it, so you should at least feel confident with your purchase decision. At this stage, I'm not suggesting you have to feel like you want to live in the property, but it's about *wanting* to own it and make it work as an investment. That means you need to have belief in the property, the area and its future potential. This belief should come first from the numbers and research you have performed, and also from your instinct for the investment – if, for whatever reason, something does not feel right, walk away. Always trust your instincts.

Get used to viewing properties and aim to see a variety of types and styles. Get a feel for the different types of housing stock and the sorts of people who live in them. Learn about the pros and cons and understand how value is created and what makes one property worth more than another. Take time to consider your options, be comfortable with the choices you make, and enjoy the process. Property is not a one-size-fits-all investment and so you should choose what you want to invest in and why. Don't rush what is likely to be one of the most important investment decisions of your

life. And don't forget – you have to kiss a lot of frogs before
you find a prince!

Go For It!

Look at the different types of property available on the market.
Take time to view a variety of different places so that you can
understand how properties vary and why.

Rule 29: There is no perfect property deal

Every deal has something that you have to compromise on.

Over the years, I have found great deals, lucrative deals, deals that looked good on paper and then turned into duds, dud deals that turned out to be good – and I've even found a few stupendous deals. But I have yet to find the *perfect* deal. Every deal has *something* that you have to compromise on. Maybe it will be the level of risk involved that keeps you awake at night, maybe it will be the price you have to pay, maybe it's about the level of work involved or the time-frame you will have to own it. Regardless of what it is, the perfect deal does *not* exist, and I would suggest you don't even bother looking for it.

Many people when they first get started in property investment are looking for the 'perfect deal' – the deal that ticks all the boxes and where everything will work out just 'perfectly'. In the real world, this just doesn't happen. You may get lucky once or twice, but, as a general rule, it's unlikely and you'll waste an awful lot of time searching for it. Deals need to make sense – they may not be perfect, but they need to make money. Making money is what you are looking to do – you are *not* looking for perfection.

Trying to find the perfect deal is a great excuse for

procrastination. It is also another good reason to buy another book, attend another talk or pay to go on another course. In the quest to secure the perfect deal, you feel you need to acquire the perfect knowledge to make it happen. But all that will actually happen is that you will spend a lot of time and money looking in the wrong place. You need to be looking for deals. Deals that make money.

You have to accept you are probably going to make some mistakes. I made quite a few in the beginning and I learned a lot from them. But mistakes, like a bad haircut, will grow out. If you have done your research and followed the Rules, it's unlikely to go so disastrously wrong. You may take a few steps back, your confidence may get knocked, but then you will get back up and try again.

Perfection is not the aim. You will have to make compromises. You will not find *exactly* what you are looking for, but, once you have found something that is 'good enough', that makes financial sense and that you feel comfortable with, then it's time to act. It's time to put your money where your mouth is and take action. Because it's when you get going that you'll *really* start learning – and that is a whole new ball game entirely!

Go For It!

Look again at a deal you have previously considered and ask yourself: what needs to be done to make the deal work?

Rule 30: Make money from 'What if?'

Potential is not always obvious to spot.

People often get fixated with buying property at a discount. Below Market Value (BMV) is a favoured term. Trying to get money off and buying at a rock-bottom price is seen as the way to make money. How to source and buy property at a discount has spawned an entire industry with books, courses, websites and a myriad of different tools on offer that claim to teach you how to spot and buy bargains. But buying cheap is just one strategy.

Another strategy for making money is to find property that has potential. It may not be priced at a discount or have a motivated vendor, and it may not even need work, but it could *still* have potential. Potential is not always obvious to spot. It may be a typical family property that could be converted to flats or a shared house. It may be a top-floor flat that has the potential to be extended into the roof. It may be a piece of garden with the possibility of planning permission. It could even be some public toilets you walk past every day on the way to work. The truth is, potential and opportunity are all around you. And I bet, if you sat for just a few minutes and thought about your local area, you would soon remember a building, a piece of land or something you have had your eye on and pondered: 'What if?'

The problem is, most people ignore the 'What if?' moments of their life. They walk by opportunities every day but don't pay attention or take the necessary action. If a property is not being advertised 'For Sale', being sold cheap or in need of work, it's classified as a 'non-opportunity'. And that is where so many people go wrong. Just because you are prepared to pay a fair market value does not mean you are overpaying; it means you are paying for the opportunity to unlock the potential. Now, when you put it like that, it sounds different, doesn't it?

Making money doesn't necessarily mean buying property for as low a price as you can and selling it for as high as you can. That's great if you can manage it every time, but investment is also about understanding the opportunity and potential on offer and paying to have access to that. Deals need to stack, but it is not a one-way street. Vendors need to feel they have also got a deal – if they haven't, they won't sell, and then you will not have any potential to unlock. Potential can come in many forms. It may not be specific to the property – it could even be knowledge you have gained about the local area, perhaps a new tube line or redevelopment plan is in the offing.

Making money in property means you need to calculate your upside (the potential) against your downside (the risk). Weighing up the upside with the downside (the risk-to-reward ratio) is how you decide if a property can make you money, and potentially what risks it may involve. It is only when you have calculated and assessed these figures that you will know if there is any money to be made.

Go For It!

Think about the 'What if?' opportunities local to you. Go and visit them and do the necessary research. If the deal stacks, track down the owner via the land registry or deliver some letters expressing your desire to buy.

Rule 31: Know your patch

The only way you can really get to know an area is by researching the statistics and spending time there.

Before you invest a load of money, it is vital you understand the area in which the property is located. Places can change – and not always for the better. Large employers can move out of an area and this can rapidly change the dynamics from one of prosperity to poverty. The loss of employment can lead to reduced spending power and hit all purses across the spectrum. This has an impact on the demand for housing and also the desire to live in an area. At the other end of the spectrum, employers moving into an area can signal a boom in its fortunes and an increase in demand to live close by.

Less tangible than the physical characteristics of a place is its 'spirit' – the outlook of the people living there. Perhaps this is best described as the 'feel' of an area. That is, the emotional response people feel to living and being in a particular place. Feelings have a financial value attached to them and people will pay more to live in an area that makes them feel good.

The only way you can really get to know an area is by researching the statistics and spending time there. Knowing the local crime statistics, employment figures and school ratings will give you a good overall idea of an area. However, you also need to get a feel for a place on a micro level by walking the streets and looking at what is happening. While walking around, you should note down the sorts of people who live in the area, the types of cars they drive, any improvements people are making, how much pride they take in their property's appearance, how clean the area is and what sorts of facilities are available. Note also any transport links, cafés, bars, shops and recreational facilities such as gyms and parks, and watch how they are used and by whom. You should check what is happening in the area by reading the local newspaper, looking for planning applications and checking local notice boards. These sources of information will give you a good insight.

Knowing your patch means identifying the best streets, worst streets, streets that have potential – and the streets that have a tendency to spoil. Intimate knowledge can be gleaned from a variety of sources, including talking with local estate agents and business owners and spending time in the local pub or café. It is really important to get to grips with an area and think to yourself: 'If I lived here, what sort of life would I have?' You need to imagine the kinds of people who live in the area and how they fit with the sort of customers you are looking to attract. By getting under the skin of the people, you will be able to understand the dynamics driving the local market and what motivates people to live there (or not!). This knowledge will enable you to purchase the right property, in the right place, for the right people.

Go For It!

Buy a street map of your patch and talk to local estate agents to pinpoint the best and worst streets. Now walk down these and write down what makes one street better than another.

Rule 32: Buy local

If you're looking for less stress and more success in your investments, it is advisable to buy local to you.

Where you invest in property is critical. This will not only dictate the future success of your investments, but will also impact upon your everyday life. If you're looking for less stress and more success in your investments, it is advisable to buy local to you. That means operating within a thirty- to forty-minute drive of your home address. This can seem a tall order if you live in a particularly expensive area or an area where there is poor demand. However, you'd be surprised how many areas of potential investment exist within a short commuting radius of your home. By inputting your postcode into property websites such as Rightmove and Zoopla and selecting within a thirty-mile radius, you will soon see the variety of other areas located within commuting distance.

Long-distance property ownership is possible; however, the distance does place a strain on your management ability. Owning property far away means you have less choice in how the property is managed and it can increase costs because you have to outsource so much of the work. This can mount up to additional financial expenses, which impact upon your bottom line. Moreover, when a property is located far away, it is often impossible to 'pop round' and this can create logistical headaches, especially when your opinion is really needed on something. All of these factors should be taken into account when considering purchasing at a distance and my advice would be, unless the property is an exceptional bargain or very special, that it is best to stick close to your local area.

Buying local also means:

- You already have an idea of the local market by virtue of living in the area. You may not be a property expert, or have analysed the market in detail; however, you will have picked up a good level of local knowledge just by living close by.

- By living locally, you are more likely to have a network of contacts you can call upon when the need arises. Even if you are new to investing in property in your area, it is likely you will know some-body who can point you in the right direction.

- Properties located nearby are often better managed. Being close by means you can conduct more frequent checks and be on hand to attend to any issues.

- Living close to your investments means they are cheaper to manage, as you can often do what's needed yourself. Even if you want to employ an agent for some tasks, the proximity of the property will mean the choice is yours to make. If you want, you can instruct, or carry out repairs yourself, and you can make viewings, or meet tenants and, ultimately, manage the property from your doorstep.

- Buying properties locally is often less of a risk. Properties that are, if you choose, close by can be checked at regular intervals, and any issues that arise can be sorted very quickly.

Go For It!

Put your home postcode into websites such as Zoopla and Rightmove and select properties for sale within a thirty-mile radius. Note down all the potential areas for investment close to where you live.

Rule 33: Know what you like and forget the rest

Knowing what you like and forgetting the rest means focusing on what you believe is the right selection for you at this moment in time.

Investing in property gives you a level of control and choice not often found with many other forms of investment. Property allows you to pick and choose where you want to invest, what you want to invest in and who you want to do business with. How successful you want to make your property investment career is down to you. The ability to be in such control of your destiny can be intoxicating. However, being in such a position of power can sometimes feel overwhelming. There are so many choices and possibilities on the market, how do you know what to do for the best?

Investment objectives and mathematical calculations can take you so far – knowing you can make money is a good start. But then what?

Choose what you like, is my advice. Personally, I go for properties that turn me on and that I *want* to own. Once I have done my research and know a property is going to make money, then it's down to me and whether I *like* the property. It's about how a property makes me *feel*: what excites me about owning the property, what worries me, what good things do I think can come of owning it, what challenges do I think may arise? Once I've run the numbers on a property, it's a very intuition-based approach – I either like it or I don't! And sometimes what you like may be very specific – it could be having a penchant for period properties, or only buying in particular streets. But it is important to remember to *like* what you buy. At the end of the day, it's your money and your investment, so it is critical you like what you buy because you'll probably own it for a while to come!

Sometimes it's difficult to define what you like, but knowing what you *don't* like is also important. Understanding the properties you don't like and the areas you won't consider enables you to have boundaries to focus on what you *do* actually like. Having these criteria enables you to be more selective in the decisions you make. Of course, criteria do not have to be set in stone and you are allowed to change your mind! There have been times when I have revisited areas that I previously disliked and found myself liking them. There have even been times when I have reconsidered areas or property types that I originally liked and found myself not liking them any more! Criteria change as you grow and as you learn more – both about property investment and also about yourself and what you like (and don't like).

Every investor has their own ideas about what a good property means to them. Your investment criteria are personal and unique to you. You have your own investment objectives, goals and ways of doing things. Knowing what you like and forgetting the rest means focusing on what you believe is the right selection for you at a given moment.

Be conscious that your criteria and choices may change as you develop and grow. But most importantly: *stick to what you like*. Trust your instincts and go with decisions that feel good. Have belief in your opinion, trust that you know what you like, and don't spend too much time dwelling on what you don't like!

Go For It!

Take a few minutes to write down a list of 'likes' and 'dislikes'. Do it off the top of your head, as this will be more instinctive. You will see a pattern emerging and this will enable you to set your criteria for your property search.

Rule 34: If it sounds too good to be true . . . it usually is!

Something is only worth what someone else is willing to pay.

I have lost count of the number of deals that looked too good to be true, led me down blind alleyways, and sucked me into cul-de-sacs of investment excitement. The sad fact is if something sounds too good to be true . . . it usually is. Every investor craves finding the diamond in the rough, the missed opportunity, the development that nobody else saw. However, on most occasions, there is usually a very good reason why something has not been done or somebody else has not yet acted on the opportunity. That is not to say they don't exist – they do – but be wary of how often you plan to find such wonderful bargains. They are rare and very few and far between.

Buying below market value or BMV is a notion that many investors will be familiar with. Trying to bag a bargain at a great discount and profiting hugely is a fantastic aim, but it is also incredibly difficult and very time-consuming. People rarely sell properties for less than they are worth and, even when their circumstances dictate the need for a quick sale, such as falling into debt or separating from a partner, it is unlikely you will purchase a property at such an incredibly reduced market value.

Properties are worth what someone is willing to pay and the value is dictated by the market. The price may be what someone wants to sell a property for, or it may be what you want to buy it for – but that is not the same as the value. Something is only worth what someone else is willing to pay. Of course, there may be occasions where a property was placed at a higher price and you managed to get a substantial sum off the asking price, but that does not mean you managed to buy BMV. There could well be something about the property that meant no one else wanted it at that price. Thus, even with your substantial discount, what you paid for the property could well be the market value of the property.

The same is also true of properties that sell in excess of their asking price. An asking price is just a number that has been placed on the property by an agent and/or the vendor; it is not the same as the market value. Value is decided and determined ultimately by the market. Thorough research, knowing your numbers, and analysing the competition and the market are the only ways to understand when something is too good to be true – or when something sounds too good but is actually true!

Go For It!

Search for a property local to you that has sold within the last six months. Check Rightmove House Prices Tool and compare the asking price with the actual sold price. Calculate the difference between asking and paid prices (remember the paid price can be higher and/or lower than the asking price).

Rule 35: Money pits vs. gold-mines

Not every property that requires work will turn a profit

Making money from a property that 'needs work' is not as easy as buying a property that 'needs work' and selling a property that '*doesn't* need work'. Not every property is a profitable enterprise and the oft-seen magical term 'requires modernisation' does not equate to 'will make you a shed load of cash'. In fact, sometimes what that means is: 'will take you a huge amount of time and money, and you would have been better off buying a property that had already been renovated'. This is the hard reality of the matter – not every property is a gold-mine.

Identifying the profit potential of a property is much harder than people think. Just because an estate agent claims a property requires work, or has 'potential', doesn't mean it's financially worthwhile. It's possible to add value to a property in many different ways, but you have to be sure you are actually going to *make* money, and that is a different thing. Adding value needs to be financially viable and it needs to be extracted as real, hard money. It is the money that ultimately matters, rather than the value that is added.

So how can you tell the difference between a money pit and a gold-mine? Both have potential to add value, but the money pit has the potential to *take* your money, whereas the gold-mine can *make* you money. On paper the two can easily be confused – both appear to be opportunities; however, the key to understanding the difference is thorough research. Research is the key to understanding when a property has profit potential and is a worthwhile financial venture. It must be remembered: not every property that requires work will turn a profit.

How you assess whether a property will make a profit is a far more scientific task than many people assume. Creativity certainly comes into the equation, but making money from property is not as simple as replacing a kitchen or changing a colour scheme. Mathematical sums are the hard and fast rules. Every cost and every item of expenditure needs to be added together and subtracted from the anticipated end value. And that end value also needs to be thoroughly researched and clarified. Contingency costs need to be included, market fluctuations accounted for and buffers built in if you are to stand a chance of making money.

To make money from property, you need to thoroughly research and identify only the *real* opportunities and potential gold-mines. The rest will be money pits and, while they may have an opportunity to add value, they will have very little chance to make any actual real money. Make the calculator your best friend and remember that adding value only matters when you're going to make money.

Go For It!

Look up a property for sale that is listed as requiring modernisation. Check the comparison figures for a property that has already been modernised. Calculate all the costs involved in buying, refurbishing and selling the unmodernised property. Work out what the potential profit may be. Is it financially worthwhile?

Rule 36: Get your values right

The quickest and easiest way to obtain a valuation is through 'comparison desk research' of properties being marketed for sale and those recently sold.

The quickest and easiest way to obtain a valuation is through 'comparison desk research' of properties being marketed for sale and those recently sold. This can be done online using property websites such as Rightmove and Zoopla. This online estimation should be further supported with expert knowledge from local agents. For a more accurate valuation, it is advisable to request a home visit from an agent.

There are five steps to obtaining an estimated desk-top property valuation:

- **Step 1:** Input the property postcode and search within a quarter-, then half-mile radius of the property. Include 'Sale/ Let Agreed' results. This will list all properties currently on the market and those that have been let or sold subject to contract. Make a note of all similar properties and record values and listing dates of when the properties were added on the site. The listing date will tell you how long a property has been available and can indicate the strength of the local market.

- **Step 2:** Select the 'Price Comparison Tool' in Rightmove. Input the property postcode and search within a quarter- and half-mile radius. The results will list all properties currently on the market, detail any price reductions and display any properties that were previously for sale but are no longer on the market. Make a note of all similar properties, values and dates.

- **Step 3:** Select the 'Sold House Prices' tool in Rightmove. Input the property postcode and search for recent house price sales. The results will list land registry data (actual transaction prices) combined with any previous Rightmove marketing listings of the property and, where applicable, will show property details including photographs and floor plans. As in the previous step, make a note of all similar properties, sold prices and dates.

- **Step 4:** Collate all selected properties from the previous three steps. Analyse the results in comparison with the property you are researching. Pay attention to any differences, such as the size, condition of the fixtures and fittings, and age and style of the kitchen and bathroom, as these will influence the value of a property. Check the floor plans for layout differences and note the size of the property in total square feet (if not on the floor plans this may be available in the Energy Performance Certificate (EPC)). Dividing the asking price by the total square feet will give you an indication of the price of the property per square foot. This data should enable you to calculate an estimated value for the property.

- **Step 5:** With the estimated value to hand, contact three local agents to check your findings. Without seeing the property, the valuations from the agent will be ball-park; however, they will give you a good idea to ensure you are on the right track. Discuss with the agents the strength of the local market based upon the listing date details you have obtained.

Following these five steps will enable you to quickly and easily estimate the value of a property.

Go For It!

Visit Rightmove and Zoopla and input your own property post-code. Follow the five steps outlined above to estimate the value. Now call three agents to check your findings.

Rule 37: You get what you pay for

Price is just one part of the equation – it's actually the service and value you are getting that comprise the other and, arguably, more important parts.

There is a huge difference between making the most of what you've got and being cheap. Being cheap is often a false economy. Trying to cut costs may save you money in the short term, but long term the 'cost saving' usually ends up costing you more. That means you always need to figure out the 'true cost' of any given expense. This applies to almost everything in the world of property.

Let's take, for example, a cheap property. Cheap properties can make good rental investments. However, they usually come with a hidden cost – time and hassle. Cheap properties tend to attract a lower quality of tenant who require more management. A cheap property will probably cost more to maintain and, while producing stronger rental yields, will most likely be a poor performer when it comes to capital growth. That's not to say this choice is wrong, but it's a case of understanding the 'true cost' implications of that investment decision.

Cheap labour is another example. It's always tempting

to opt for the lowest quote; however, it's imperative you ask why a quote is so low. Usually it will be because the standard of the workmanship is not so high, or maybe because the builder has a sting in the tail with some added extras at the end. Or maybe the project will not be completed in the time-frames you set. Maybe the cheap quote will work out and everything proves fine and dandy, but, in my experience, normally the cheapest quote comes with some sort of strings attached. This is fine – you just need to know what those strings are.

Staying with property maintenance and repairs, there's often a desire to do some jobs yourself – even if you're not skilled at them. You think about the savings you can make by doing this, but you forget to take into consideration the time it will take you – time that could be spent doing something else. Moreover, have you thought about the finish of the job afterwards? Will your finish be good enough to get you the money you were hoping to get – or would it have been better to employ a professional and get a professional finish, which you could then charge more for?

The same principle applies to using sales and letting agents. I know many investors who shop around on price and choose agents because of the lower fees they charge. The bottom line is what they become fixated on. But the bottom line is dependent upon your selecting an agent who is the *best* for the job. The best agent will tend to earn their higher fees back in spades – they will achieve more money for a property and do so in a shorter time-frame. The price is just one part of the equation – it's actually the service and value you are getting that comprise the other and, arguably, more important parts.

Go For It!

Think about a service you value; for example, your broadband connection. Is the price the only thing you consider, or are there other factors such as reliability and good customer service that play a part? Understand how service and value for money can influence your decisions.

Rule 38: Understand types of property ownership

Freehold is the outright ownership of the property and the land on which it stands. Leasehold is the ownership of the property, but not the land it stands on.

In the UK there are two main ways of owning property: Freehold and Leasehold.

Freehold is very simple: outright ownership of the property and the land on which it stands. Freeholds tend to mainly be houses. There is no time limit to the ownership and it can be passed to your heirs. Owning a Freehold property means that, within planning regulations, you can do what you want to the property, such as extending it to make it larger. As the freeholder you are responsible for the maintenance and repair of the property. Freehold properties tend to be more valuable and desirable than Leasehold properties.

Leasehold is the ownership of a property, but not the land it stands on. Apartments and flats are usually owned on a Leasehold basis. A Leasehold means you own the property for a fixed number of years according to the length of the lease you buy. The lease is a legal agreement between the freeholder (also known as the landlord), who owns the land on which the property sits, and the owner of the lease, who is known as the leaseholder.

Lease lengths vary, although most have terms of 99 or 125 years. It is important to note with a Leasehold property that the term of the lease does not start again when you buy or sell. For example, if you buy a property in 2014 that has a ninety-nine-year lease, and the lease began in the year 2000, fourteen years would already have expired and so you could only retain ownership for the remaining eighty-five years. When the lease term expires, possession of the property passes back to the freeholder. This means that, as the length of the lease shortens, the value reduces: it is a 'diminishing asset'. Usually the lease can be extended by agreement with the freeholder and a premium will be paid for the extension. Leases under eighty years are generally more expensive to extend because of the premium known as 'Marriage Value' – this is where the freeholder also shares in the increased value of the Leasehold property with an extended lease. Short leases can often be difficult to raise finance on, but can present interesting investment opportunities for cash-rich investors.

Leasehold properties often have covenants relating to the responsibilities of a leaseholder. You will usually need to get permission to make alterations to the property and will need to make additional payments to the freeholder. For example, Ground Rent is an annual payment that is in effect a rent in return for allowing the property to stand on the freeholder's land. This Ground Rent can vary from a peppercorn to sometimes thousands of pounds per year. It is usually fixed and increases every twenty-five years. The freeholder is also responsible for the maintenance and upkeep of the building and, as a leaseholder, you will be required to pay a service charge. Service charges can vary considerably and are the cause of many disputes. Some freeholders may also employ a managing agent to look after the building and this fee will usually be added to the service charge.

Leaseholders can gain more control of a building by exercising their 'Right to Manage' (RTM). This can be done without the landlord's consent or a need to prove 'mismanagement', although at least 50 per cent of the leaseholders will have to participate. A further option is for 'Collective Enfranchisement', which is where leaseholders buy a share of the Freehold. Flats with a share of the Freehold are usually more valuable and desirable.

Go For It!

Search for some short Leasehold properties for sale (i.e. less than seventy years). Call the estate agents and find out how much the property would be worth with a longer lease (i.e. ninety-nine years). Calculate the difference those years make to a property's value.

Rule 39: Age *does* matter

The age of a property has a great bearing on the capital value – and also the upkeep costs.

Over half of the housing stock in the UK dates from 1850 onwards. The Victorians were prolific house builders and we owe much of our current housing supply to our ancestors' property development skills. Typically, home buyers tend to favour properties that are either old and full of character or modern new-build. Properties built after 1945 and which are not new-build tend to have less market appeal, and many design styles of the 1960s/70s are seen as too boxy and plain by today's standards. This means that much of the 'middle market' – i.e. those properties built between 1945 and 1995 – tend to be less valued as they lack period charm or modern convenience.

The age of a property has a great bearing on its capital value – and also its upkeep costs. If you intend to invest long term, the running and maintenance expenses of different property types need to be taken into consideration. New-build properties are often favoured by investors who are looking for minimal maintenance. However, it is important to note the depreciation of new-builds, which can take some time to recoup. This is similar to the depreciation often found in the new car market, where a car loses a substantial part of its value simply because it is no longer new. Properties also command a premium for being new.

However, unlike cars, although new-build properties may initially depreciate, appreciation usually kicks back in again!

Buying off-plan can be a way to obtain new-builds at a potential discount. But it is worth bearing in mind the difficulties in valuing the end product, plus the risk of a development being delayed or unfinished. Development release dates are also key because, if too many units are released at the same time, the market risks being flooded, which can lead to over-supply and falling rents. Moreover, with this type of property, commoditisation is more likely to occur due to the lack of differentiation. Potentially, this can lead to future price wars.

Victorian terraces are well loved by tenants and investors alike. They offer spacious and charming living accommodation and there is plentiful choice on the market. However, Victorian properties require constant maintenance and repair to ensure they remain of a good standard. I have found they typically suffer from damp, thin party walls and lack of adequate insulation. This can make them quite expensive to upkeep – even after a comprehensive scheme of modernisation.

Apartments are often favoured by investors who are looking to gain a cheap foothold on the market. These types of properties can work well, especially in high-demand locations; however, the long-term costs associated with a Leasehold such as Ground Rent and service charges should be taken into account, as these can take a major chunk of any potential monthly profits.

Age matters when it comes to property investment and you should bear in mind upkeep and maintenance costs to ensure your figures stack both now and in the future.

Go For It!

Compare the prices of a 1970s-built house and a 1900s-built house. What price difference do you see?

Rule 40: Convenience sells

Most people want to be close to
something or someone.

Few people want to live in the middle of nowhere. Only a minority of people aspire to be hermits. Most want to be close to something or someone. People want to be able to get out and get on, not have to trek to the supermarket, spend ages getting to work or be miles away from anyone and anything else. People want to be private and have their own space – but they want to be connected and within reach of things. They want an easy life. *Convenience sells*.

If you don't believe me, just check the prices of properties that are close to a train or tube station. You'll see that the price for those located nearby is far higher than those more than a ten-minute walk away. People want to be close to transport routes. Transport connections mean you can get somewhere else, and everybody at some point will need or want to travel. But here's the rub: you need to be connected to transport, but you can't be 'on top' of it. Railway lines and motorways at the rear of a property do not command a premium. That is when convenience becomes *inconvenience* and devalues your property.

The same is true of being close to shops, bars, restaurants and schools. It is very convenient when these facilities are located nearby, preferably within a ten-minute walk, but you don't want to be neighbours. You don't want to live next door to the pub or the shop, even if they are your favourite places. Being too close drops the value. All those customers passing in and out all the time create too much traffic and you don't want that on your doorstep or right outside your window.

Having extra space is massively convenient – both indoors and outdoors. People have a lot of stuff and so extra storage is always appreciated. It makes their life easier. They don't have to throw away stuff, nor do they even have to think about it. Having a place for a car is a bonus – even if it is on-street and you need to pay for a permit. Most people like to be able to have cars, even if they don't need them. Cars are useful and when a property has parking it makes having a car even more so. People like to have the choice. If you haven't got space for a car, at least show them you have space to store a bike. Bikes too are a convenient way to get around.

Choose places that have outside space, or which at least have the potential for it. If you're in a city, it doesn't have to be big – even a fire escape will do. Grow flowers and strategically place pots to make the outside space a part of your property. Make the outside feel a part of the inside – it will make it feel bigger and give the illusion that you own more.

Investing in property that is conveniently located will always be in demand. People want an easy life, but they want to have choices. Choices are good – they give people options. When you buy a conveniently located property and make it convenient for people to live in, you will be giving yourself the best chance to make some *conveniently* easy money!

Go For It!

Check the prices of properties close to nearby transport connections such as railway stations and tube stations. Calculate the premium these properties command for being located nearby. Work out what the price drop-off distance is. How much extra does being one-minute closer add?

Rule 41: Buy something special

Properties that have that 'something special'
usually command a price premium and
tend to be more saleable.

There are millions of properties for sale and rent, and people have masses of choice about where to live. So it's important to buy a property that has 'something special' about it. This doesn't mean you need to buy a converted water mill or something of that ilk, but it does mean you have to look for the unique selling point (USP) of a property. You need to look for something about the property that sets it apart from the competition: a point of difference, a reason why somebody would choose *your* property over another.

Trying to find something special in a property takes time and can be hard work. Sometimes that 'something special' in a property may not be there from the outset and you have to create it. However, the most important thing is that it exists (or will exist) and other people can see it too. There must be a credible and valued reason why your property would be chosen over another. This 'something special' is your property's USP and it is at the very heart of how to invest successfully. Properties that have that 'something special' stand head-and-shoulders above the rest and tend to outperform the market because of their USP.

USPs can be both property specific and location specific. For example, a property may be located in a particularly sought-after area, or may benefit from a point of difference such as original period features, or a particularly large, private garden. USPs don't have to be incredibly rare, but they do have to be relevant and have meaning and value to the audience. This can be anything from having a garage, to the potential to extend, to having sea views or the most jaw-dropping kitchen design. USPs create a platform that you can sell from and that enable you to maximise your investment. For example, a property with original period features that has been modernised sympathetically is likely to command more money than a period property where all the features have been stripped out.

Properties that have that 'something special' usually command a price premium and tend to be more saleable. That means you should look for a point of difference and locate the unique quality of any property you invest in. By understanding what has relevance, appeal and value in the marketplace, you will be able to make the most of your investment. So, dare to be different, look for USPs and make your investment choices based upon what *more* you can offer to the marketplace.

Go For It!

Go on Rightmove and/or Zoopla and check the properties for sale locally to you. List those that jump out at you and the reasons why. Go and see your top three favourites and confirm if the USPs deliver in reality.

Rule 42: Check demand before you buy

Understanding the dynamics of local demand and any particular patterns of your target audience needs to be built into your decision making.

In the heat of the moment and the excitement of finding a potential property deal, it's easy to get carried away. However, before you part with a penny, you need to ensure you have done all your homework and checked there is sufficient demand before you buy. This is a critical test that will show you if the property you intend to purchase is likely to be a good investment.

Testing market demand can be done in a number of ways. Property websites such as Rightmove and Zoopla will give you a good indication of the available stock. This information can be further drilled down to check the demand levels. One way of doing this is by using the 'date listed' detail of any similar properties. This information is often available on the property adverts displayed in Zoopla. By knowing the date the property was first listed and calculating the length of time it took to sell or rent, this will provide you with an indication of how fast (or slow) the market is moving, and the levels of demand locally. This information should be further honed by calling the agents to discuss the details in more depth.

Market research for rental properties via test ads is a great way to identify demand levels and estimate how successful a particular investment may be. On many occasions, especially when I am looking at investing in a new area, I have placed a test ad on the major websites to assess the interest levels. I use an external shot of the property and write the details, including the rent I anticipate to achieve. I evaluate the different enquiries I receive and the questions asked to form my thinking further. I also use this test as an opportunity to explore any issues or challenges that I may not have previously considered. This can range from questions with regards to parking arrangements to the internal layout of the kitchen. This allows me to gain real market knowledge and gives me an insight into how the property is likely to perform when placed on the market.

Understanding the dynamics of local demand and any particular patterns of your target audience needs to be built into your decision making. For example, if you are looking to invest in a student property, it is critical to know the term dates, when students start looking and what group size is preferred. The knowledge you glean will enable you to understand if the proposed property meets the target group demand. By testing and analysing a property on the market, it enables you to gain insights into your target market before you commit to buy. Knowing and being sure there is demand is critical if you are to succeed.

Go For It!

Visit the Zoopla website, input your postcode and search for properties to rent within your local area, making sure you've included 'Let Agreed'. Note down the listing dates of the properties and calculate the length of time it took to rent the property. Now do the same for properties listed 'For Sale'. What does the data suggest about demand levels in your local area?

Rule 43: Be a Nosy Parker

Your job is to get to the bottom of why the property you are considering buying would make a good investment.

Being a 'Nosy Parker' is not the usual ambition for most investors – but being *overly* inquisitive is a useful and effective skill in discovering great properties. Diligent and continuous questions should be asked of all investment decisions; it is only by challenging your assumptions that you can develop better and more robust strategies for the future.

Being nosy often conjures up images of meddlers and people who like to interfere. However, I think a more apt analogy would be that of a detective: *a property detective*. In this guise, your role as an investigator can be more fully appreciated – your job is to get to the bottom of why the property you are considering buying would make a good investment.

So how can you find out this information by being nosy?

Most importantly, you need to be interested. You need to want to know what an area is like, how a property may be lived in, what changes are happening, what people live in the street, what sorts of jobs they do – where and how they commute, shops they shop at, schools their children go to, bars and restaurants they like visiting and all the rest of the shebang that goes into being interested in how and why people live the lives they do. And you need to apply all of that knowledge to the property you are intending to purchase.

Taking time to walk around an area and talk to neighbours and local business owners is paramount for you to get the inside story on an area. Don't be afraid to strike up conversations with people who live in the street – knock on the door if you have to. Talk to them, tell them you are thinking of buying a property in the area and would like to know more. Ask and you will find out – people love to talk and they adore being asked to give an opinion. Look through people's windows, notice the décor they have, check out the cars they drive, how they maintain their property, what their gardens look like, how clean is the street, are there any neighbourhood watch schemes? Check the local postcards displayed in the shops – what sorts of things are people selling, what community activities are available?

Spend time people-watching. Grab a drink at a local café or pub and watch the world go by. Note down the sorts of people who are passing by: the types of clothes they are wearing, bags they are carrying, speed at which they are walking. What clues can you deduce from the local population? Look around you and take in as much as you can. Be a sponge. Absorb all this information so that you can process it into your investment decision. And don't be afraid to ask difficult questions – be prepared for some hard truths and build them into your knowledge bank. Knowing the inside story enables you to draw wiser and better conclusions.

Go For It!

Visit a local café in an area you have not been to before. Sit and people-watch. Note down what you see. Talk to other people in the café about what the area is like, find out what people love and hate about the place.

Rule 44: Don't take it personally . . .

You are creating a home for somebody else.

Buying a property to refurbish is hugely exciting. You have so many ideas, things you want to get on with and can't wait to get started.

But wait. Stop! If this is a property for you to let out or sell on, then you must get more businesslike and have to stop taking it so personally. Unless you are going to live in the property, you are now creating a product for *someone else*. That means you need to think about who you hope will buy or rent the property from you.

This is one of the hardest things so many investors have to overcome from the start: it may be your property, but actually it's a product designed for your customers and it will be their home. The sooner you start thinking like a product owner, the better off you will be and the more money you will have in your pocket. Plus, the more success-ful you will be.

So what does it mean to think like a product owner? First you need to understand your customer. What makes them tick? What is it about your product they will want to buy? What features can it offer them? How does it benefit them? What makes your product better than the competition? If you don't know the answers to these questions, you must start doing some research now to know what your customer is looking for.

Preparing a property for sale or rent means creating a home where somebody wants to live. Your role is to create that impression of a perfect home for your target audience. It's the same thinking that goes into the show homes that developers use to sell properties that are not yet built. People need a display model where they can imagine themselves living, and be able to put themselves into the shoes of the person who would live there. They need to feel there is, or could be, a fit between their lifestyle and the new home they are looking at. They want and need to feel they are a part of the property – and building that connection with your audience is what you need to aim for.

If you are to sell or rent your property successfully, you need to get under the skin of your potential customers. You need to research and plan how they would live at the property and then make it for them. It is critical to always remember that, while it may be your property, it will be somebody else's home, and for that very reason you have to make it for them. Not you.

Go For It!

Write a customer profile of your target buyer/renter. Think about how old they are, their family arrangements (married/single/co-habiting/kids), where they work, how much they earn, what they like doing in their leisure time, what are they looking for from a property. For example, do they need to be close to schools, somewhere to park the car, a large kitchen to eat in? Put yourself in the shoes of your customer and look again at your property – are you making it a home for them? What features will it offer them and what benefits will they gain?

Rule 45: Add value in areas that are valued

The value added should be at least
double the cost of the works.

When a property needs work, it's very easy to get carried away and think you need to do *everything*. And some properties do need *everything* doing to get them back into a habitable state. However, before you pile in and start stripping everything back to brick, you need to ask yourself: 'am I adding value?'

In the world of property only certain things add value, and some areas add more value than others. The trick to successful property investment is in understanding *where* to add value. What is it about your property that people value – or will value? Properties are not built equally and what is important in one property may not be as important in another. You need to take the time to understand how your target market, property and location fit together to ensure you get the most out of your investment.

So how best to add value? You need to start by identifying those areas that people value and work out a priority order for them. Every property requires a modern, functioning kitchen and bathroom, but which of these adds more value? What is more important to your audience? Which area takes priority? The same goes for finishes and the quality of the fixtures and fittings and the type of wall and floor coverings. Real hardwood flooring may be expected and required in some properties, whereas with others a good-quality laminate wood floor will add just as much value.

By analysing the priority aspects of a property that people are attracted to, you can add value in areas that are valued. Woodchip wallpaper in the lounge may not be the first choice of many people; however, if this is a property for rental you have to ask yourself: how much value will changing that wallpaper add? Even if the property is intended as a re-sale, you have to calculate how much it will cost you to undertake the work versus how much value will be added to the end product. How much does the woodchip detract or deter from the sale of the property? What other areas of the property are valued – is it really the wallpaper in the lounge that people will be prioritising or can you spend that money in other areas such as upgrading the kitchen to achieve more value?

When faced with a refurbishment project it's easy to convince yourself you can do everything – and, given unlimited time and money, everything and anything *is* possible. However, you need to remember that property investment is a business – and it needs to make money if you are to remain in business. This means you need to focus on those areas that are of value and spend the most in those areas.

A good rule of thumb to follow is that the value added should be at least *double* the cost of the works. That means, if it costs £1,000 to remove the woodchip wallpaper in the lounge, you should anticipate the new smooth walls should add at least £2,000 to the end value of the property. Of course, you may argue that's more to do with saleability; however, you need to be clear that you're investing money to make more money, rather than spending money for the sake of it.

Go For It!

Write down the three areas that are your property's key selling points. Prioritise them and work out which one will be your star performer and which will be the supporting acts.

Rule 46: Get a grip on the domino effect

The simplest of tasks can easily and quickly snowball into the most complicated and costliest of affairs.

Changing or upgrading one part of a property may seem like a simple and straightforward affair. However, just like a giant game of dominoes, touching one part of a property impacts on other areas. Before you know it, the simplest of tasks can easily and quickly snowball into the most complicated and costliest of affairs. This is the 'domino effect' and it's important to get your head around this before you undertake any work in a property.

Changing a discoloured or out-of-date kitchen sink may seem like a small task. It's easy to buy a new kitchen sink and replace the new with the old. That's what the logical side of your brain would say. And to all intents and purposes that's correct. However, this one simple task is actually a minefield and can set in motion a whole set of consequences and added expenditure that the original task of 'changing the kitchen sink' did not foresee – unless you understand the 'domino effect'.

The 'domino effect' of changing the kitchen sink is: unless you replace the sink with exactly the same size sink, you will need to replace the worktop. Unless the pipework to the new sink is exactly the same as the one you are replacing it with, you will need to fork out for plumbing changes. Plumbing changes then come with their own set of consequences, and it's not unlikely that problems will crop up with regards to the stop-tap or some other unforeseen issue such as the connector tap or a joint or elbow. Even after you've overcome the installation of the sink, problems may well arise when it comes to trying to reinstall the tap – and you will usually end up with a new tap as well – which will also come with its own set of issues!

The reality is: your property is one large domino game. Trying to do work on one part will affect another related part. And it doesn't matter which you try to do work on – there will always be another affected part, which in turn will bring with it another set of consequences and costs. Trying to do one simple task, no matter how seemingly straightforward and unrelated, will create other issues. It will give rise to more things and more added costs. There's no getting around it – it's one of the Rules of property. So you need to ask yourself: do I really want to set this game in motion?

Once you get a grip on the 'domino effect', it will open your eyes as to why some seemingly simple tasks should be considered differently. It will guide you to understand how to budget better and plan for works in a different way. Nothing is ever as straightforward and easy as it appears, and the sooner you get a handle on how and why this is, the better prepared you will be for undertaking any apparently easy tasks.

Go For It!

Plan a simple task with the 'domino effect' in mind. Think about the dependencies of that task and all the possible consequences that could arise. Plan the additional time and money that the 'domino effect' could have.

Rule 47: Dress to impress

A property is not just shelter – a collection of bricks and tiles that keep off the rain and shield us from the cold – it is a symbol of us and who we are.

People buy with their eyes. If you want to sell or rent a property, you need to make it attractive. You need to make it look like that person can move in and start living their dream life now. Whatever else you do with your property, make sure it looks good. Good-looking properties always sell. And I know at this stage you are going to toss up the whole price-tag issue, but let me tell you, people will always pay more for a property that looks good. Attractive properties command a premium. Designer finishes sell for more. Home staging works. It may sound shallow, but the truth is, presentation is everything.

Interior design is a massive business. Show homes sell bits of scrubland yet to be built. Ikea room displays sell flat-pack bits of chipboard yet to be built. Glossy magazine features show what can be built and a dozen television programmes show us how we could have built it. Everywhere you look, design inspiration is there for the taking. And people expect it.

Unless you are selling or renting a wreck, people want and need to be impressed. Details matter. Property is not just somewhere to live – it is a statement of style. It is a part of us, a projection of our personality, our identity and how we live. Our home is unique to us – or at least we like to think it is. They say 'home is where the heart is', but it's also where the head is. Our home needs to make us feel good about ourselves. A property is not just shelter – a collection of bricks and tiles that keep off the rain and shield us from the cold – it is a symbol of us and who we are.

Presentation matters. The home you choose says a lot about you, who you are and how you want to live your life. Opting for, or feeling, second best is not a preferred option. You want to feel that your choice is unique and special to you. You want to be happy and to make this property your home; a part of your dream life. Successful property investment bottles that dream and paints it all over the property until it is dripping with it. Know your market, know their dreams, build it for them – and dress to impress!

Go For It!

Buy an interior homes magazine and look at the different lifestyles they present. Understand the varying styles used to attract people. What dream life would your target market aspire to?

Rule 48: Have a crystal ball

*Having a long-term vision and planning
what the future holds are key elements
to successful property investment.*

I know it may sound ludicrous to suggest you can see into the future – as though you are some sort of 'Mystic Meg'. However, being able to predict the future, having a long-term vision and planning what the future holds are key elements to successful property investment. Not only do you need to consider the property itself, you also need to consider the area where it is located, the wider market forces and your longer-term time-frames and goals. A consideration of these factors should have a major influence on your investment decisions – and will enable you to 'see' into the future.

Having a crystal ball requires you to have conducted a lot of research. Before you even begin to think about buying a property, you need to have identified the areas where you should invest. Every investor is different in terms of the locations they choose and this will most likely vary according to where you live, your budget, your goals, your appetite for risk and your 'get out' plan. It is critical you know at the outset your 'exit' plan as this will influence the type of property you buy and where it is located. Of course, your intention may be to never sell and pass it on to your heirs, but all of these factors should be considered.

Knowing where to invest is as critical as knowing what to invest in. The only way you can predict the future of an area is by conducting location-specific research. Local knowledge is king when it comes to foreseeing the future of an area. It is essential the local plans at the council are studied so that you are aware of any anticipated changes now and in the future. The opening of a new transport connection, new employer moving in or redevelopment of a site may have a major impact upon the location and value of your property.

Checking local planning applications will also give you an insight into the direction in which an area is heading. For example, your research may reveal a number of large properties that have had planning applications approved to convert to smaller individual dwellings. This may suggest the composition of the population is changing, which may filter through to other parts of the market. Legwork is also required and, in addition to walking the streets, it is advisable to talk to local estate agents and business owners in the area. Finding out their thoughts and opinions of an area and any changes they have experienced, or are experiencing, will give you first-hand insight.

Timing is crucial and it is important to understand the dynamics of an area and when certain future plans have already been priced into the value of a property. Areas that are set to undergo radical changes soon attract investor interest and thus it is prudent to buy as early as possible before the scheduled improvements have a major influence on the price. Analysis of land registry records provides a good indication of how prices are moving and what, if any, additional value has started to be built in to property transactions. These price points should then be set within the market context and where you believe future values may lie.

This is not an exact science and trying to call the market is incredibly difficult – however, with research and preparation you at least have the makings of a crude crystal ball!

Go For It!

Check your local council website and look for any development plans they have for the area. Read the local news (this can be done online) and Google the area. Are there any opportunities that may arise from future planned changes?

Rule 49: Don't peak too soon

The best way to avoid peaking too soon is to plan your property investment.

Unless you're on a short-term buy-to-sell strategy, property investment is a long game to play. The Rules of playing a long-term game mean you need to pace yourself. This is rather like the fable of The Tortoise and the Hare, which I am sure you will know: over-exertion and misplaced confidence is a sure-fire way to lose the game, whereas slow and steady wins the race. The reason why slow and steady is a winning strategy is precisely because *pace* is needed to withstand the course. The cyclical nature of the property market means you will need to be prepared for the long-haul journey. This requires stamina and staying power if you are to sustain your resources across a long period of time.

The importance of timing in property investment cannot be underestimated. Those who time their transactions well are those who make the most money. Admittedly, trying to time the market is an incredibly difficult feat – however, with research and a dash of luck it is possible. Having time on your side is a critical part of the game plan. It is often those investors who are forced to sell who end up losing. To remain in the game, you always need to ensure you build in extra time. This also means that any mistakes you may make in your investment career grow out. Time really is a great healer – even in the property market.

The best way to avoid peaking too soon is to plan your property investment well. That means calculating how long you intend to own a property and what you intend to do with it. It is about knowing your 'exit plan' from the start and all the different stages of the investment. This is even more important when you are planning on buying a property that requires refurbishment. Properties can be refurbished to varying standards and, while the local market will dictate much of what you are required to do, it is critical you assess any planned works within the context of the bigger picture.

Not planning, or failing to stage works over defined time periods, is an error I have seen made by many investors. To get the most amount of 'bang for your buck', it is advisable to plan refurbishment works for maximum impact. Therefore, if you plan to rent a property for the long term, it is wise to hold back on high-end finishes until you are ready to sell. Gloss worktops and designer taps can look very stylish; however, they're unlikely to add any additional value to the rent, and are all too likely to create even more maintenance issues!

Rental properties inevitably suffer wear and tear over the years and, within a remarkably short period, take on that 'lived in', 'used' feeling – regardless of how much money was spent on the renovation. For example, carpets can quickly lose their original lustre and kitchen units soon collect a huge variety of stains. To regain the 'premium' of a newly refurbished property and enhance the value of the end product, it is best practice plan and allow for additional improvements *before* placing it for sale. By doing this, you will ensure you maximise your investment – and get a top-dollar price for a 'show home'.

Go For It!

Research your local market and calculate what the premium is for a newly renovated property versus a 'used' property.

Rule 50: You will grow out of your mistakes

A bad property deal is like a bad haircut;

in time, it always grows out.

I once heard somebody say: 'A bad property deal is like a bad haircut; in time, it always grows out.' And that sums up property investment well. Mistakes happen, but, given enough time, they grow out. That doesn't mean to say they are right or that you don't have to work as hard, but it's comforting to know that in the end (if you can hang on that long!) most investment errors even out. It's also fortunate, because most people, no matter how careful they are, will at some point make a mistake in their property investment career.

Mistakes can vary in terms of scale and size – they can be anything from buying the wrong house in the wrong street, to buying the wrong property for the type of tenant you want to attract, to paying too much for a property in the first place. These mistakes may sound easy to avoid, but the truth is, areas evolve, your objectives change and the property you bought that used to attract the right sort of tenant may now attract the wrong sort of tenant. This is one of the risks of property investment – you only have so much control. Your property, and how you present it and tenant it, is within your scope of control. However, who lives next door (unless you own it) will very much be beyond your control. The same is true for the rest of the street or the surrounding area. This is why sometimes properties that initially seemed a good purchase can, over time, appear to have been a mistake.

What is always important to remember is the market is cyclical. Prices go up and down, move fast and slow, and much of this will depend upon the local and wider property market. However, usually – if you can wait long enough – the cycle will move around again to favour you once more. Moreover, given the demand for housing and people's basic need of somewhere to live, a property is unlikely to lose *all* of its value. Unlike a share, a property does not become worthless; it may not be worth as much as you paid for it, or what you hoped, but it always retains *some* value.

Unless a property has become completely unmanageable, or is haemorrhaging funds so heavily, the best thing to do on a bad buy that is set to lose you money is to wait for the market to return. Putting a property into 'tick-over' means you look to make the best of the situation and try to retain control of the asset until the market improves. The 'recovery' model of asset management means looking at potential alternative uses for the property, such as converting it into a shared house, or perhaps even taking a major rent reduction to ensure occupation until an eventual sale. This method can buy you time rather than crystallising your capital losses. On the other hand, if you have any equity in a property, it is worthwhile considering if those funds could be put to better use in an alternative investment. Losses are never welcome. However, they should not be at the expense of a potential profit elsewhere.

Bad haircuts, in time, grow out – but they need patience and maybe a little bit of styling to get them back on track.

Bad property deals are often the same – they just tend to need a few more years to grow out!

Go For It!

Plan how much money you would need to put a property into 'tick-over'. Calculate the costs you may incur from a rent reduction and how you would fund the gap.

PART THREE: BUSINESS RULES

To achieve success in property investment it must be run as a business. Even if you dabble in property or treat it as a hobby, you need to be sure you are investing in property rather than just spending money on property. Business Rules ensure you are running your property investment as a business – and making the most of the assets you have, or want to have. Everybody will have their own way of how they want to do business, but there are some key principles and Rules that are fundamental to achieving your goals. Business, like life, doesn't always run smoothly, but abiding by the Rules will increase your chances of success.

So take time to work on your business skills, plan what you want to achieve and let's get you started with being the business person you need to be.

Rule 51: It's about what you do with what you've got

Properties are not always assets, they can be liabilities.

Money does not magically flow from just owning property – management and business acumen need to be applied. In the world of everyday business, success is about *real* money. It's about the size of your profit margins and the amount of money you are making. Potential is great, future anticipated profits are wonderful, equity is fabulous – but have you ever tried to pay for a gas bill with equity or potential? You'll struggle, because most people want paying in real money, not paper money. Successful property investment is about ensuring assets *remain* assets, and that they make money. Properties can become liabilities – they go wrong, need money to maintain and can lose value. Careful asset management is required to ensure assets do not become liabilities.

Owning lots of property for the sake of *owning lots of property* is vanity. Proactive property asset management is the key to success – and you don't need to own loads to be financially free. The key is in *what you do with what you've got* – even just a few well-selected properties that are carefully managed can produce an income way beyond many people's day jobs. Just imagine owning a couple of mortgage-free houses in central London and I think you will start to get my gist. Now, let's imagine if you were to take a pro-active asset management approach. What this means is that you would be looking at all the angles to fulfil the potential, sweat the equity in the property and maximise the income you can derive. For example, maybe you would look at splitting the property into smaller units, or seeing if you could multi-let the house on a shared basis. This may have the potential to increase your income streams while still retaining the same asset. This line of thinking means you maximise the assets you have, rather than trying to add more property to the pot and potentially increasing your exposure to future liabilities.

Success comes from selecting the right assets and managing them effectively to ensure you maximise your investment. Assets need to be sweated, loan arrangements need to be analysed, and any potential needs to be looked for in every inch of the deal. Owning lots of property doesn't always equate to making lots of money, but time spent actively and effectively managing a portfolio will reap rewards. So focus your efforts on managing and making the most of what you've got, because that is the bottom line of business success, not how big your portfolio is.

Go For It!

Look at a property deal and analyse how you could maximise your return further. Is there an opportunity to increase your income streams by subdividing or extending the property? Could you refinance the property to a more competitive loan rate? Look for ways to reduce outgoings and increase your income.

Rule 52: You need more than you think

The deposit required is just the beginning.

The purchase price you pay for a property is just the start of a long list of expenses you will incur. Costs for investing soon mount up and the deposit required is only the beginning. There are many additional costs that you need to budget for, including:

- **Stamp Duty Land Tax (SDLT):** This is a tax charged on land and property transactions in the UK and is payable upon sale completion. This tax is charged at different thresholds and the starting rate of 1 per cent kicks in at £125,000 all the way up to 15 per cent for purchases over £2 million.

- **Solicitor's fees:** The cost of conveyancing work will vary according to the value of the property and the amount of work required. Typically a Leasehold property will cost more in legal fees than a Freehold property because the solicitor will have to spend more time inspecting a lease. In addition to the solicitor's fees, there are also various disbursements that need to be paid and that will be added to the final bill along with VAT.

- **Finance costs:** Raising finance costs a lot of money and it's not just about the monthly or final interest paid on the loan. Additional expenses such as the initial loan arrangement fee, administration fee, security fee and redemption fee, along with a whole host of other charges, can quickly mount up. It is vital to check the small print of any loan agreement to ensure all charges are accounted for in the total cost for finance.

- **Survey:** The cost of a survey, whether organised by the lender for a mortgage valuation or for your own purposes, will add up to several hundreds of pounds, and this needs to be accounted for.

- **Insurance:** Landlord insurance is required for any property intended to be let. This insurance is more expensive than usual homeowner cover, but it has additional cover for your legal liabilities. It is important to note that if the property is empty for more than thirty days the level of cover will usually reduce, and the premiums may rise to reflect the increased risk. You should also inform your insurer of any planned works to the property.

- **Refurbishment:** Any improvements or upgrades need to be factored in from the outset. These works will not only cost money to undertake, but the time element should also be budgeted for. While a property is being refurbished, you will not be receiving an income and you will also be liable for any utility bills. This loss of income and the additional expenses need to be taken into account.

Property investment is a capitally intensive business. Planning what money is needed above and beyond the purchase deposit is critical to ensuring you have enough to start the venture successfully.

Go For It!

List all the additional costs of buying a property and calculate how much extra is required to complete the purchase successfully.

Rule 53: Investment is a gradual business

Accumulating property is a long game, but, given time and the right investments, the cash your assets will start to generate will enable you to live the life you want to lead in the future.

Property investment demands capital and, unless you have a large pile of cash or find a joint venture partner, your progress will be constrained by how much money you have access to. This is the key stumbling block and frustration of many investors – lack of upfront capital. I'm sorry to say, there is no magic bullet to fix this. The fact is, property investment needs money. Ignore the claims some people make about 'no money down', 'lease options' or any other such 'creative way' to buy a property – you do need *some* money. While it is possible to leverage investments via mortgage lending, banks will still require you to supply a deposit. Moreover, if you are letting a property, you will also need access to funds to ensure the smooth everyday running of the tenancy.

People often get demoralised when they begin investing in property, as it can feel like you're not getting anywhere fast. In the early days, any money a property makes will likely be required to feed the business – either by improving a current asset or by acquiring more. However, by reinvesting that cash, you are growing your business into a stronger, more valuable entity with the potential to make more money in the future. Building a business takes time and it may take almost a decade for you to get where you want to be.

The best way to grow your business is to keep your personal expenses as low as possible and save as much capital as you can to invest. That means minimising the mortgage payments/rent on your own home and kissing goodbye to expensive cars, toys and holidays (see Rules 24 and 25). All of these personal expenses will massively impact upon your business because you are spending money now, which you could be investing for the future.

Accumulating property is a long game, but, given time and the right investments, the cash your assets will start to generate will enable you to live the life you want to lead in the future. Investments take time to mature, which is why it's critical you choose properties with healthy cash flow, which can sustain you while the underlying asset is gradually appreciating. Making money out of property is not an overnight lottery win – but it should be remembered that, by investing right today, you can have more tomorrow.

Go For It!

Check your personal expenses and tot up how much you spend on discretionary items. Work out what you can trim and start a savings plan to build a property purchase pot.

Rule 54: Cash flow is king

Cash flow is essential to solvency
and crucial to survival.

There is an old adage in business: 'turnover is vanity, profit is sanity, but cash is reality'. In the world of property investment: cash flow is king. Cash flow, in simple terms, is the movement of money into or out of a business, for example, the rents received in and the mortgage loans paid out. People often get hung up on profitability – but cash flow is just as important. Cash flow is a measure of a business's liquidity, and being profitable does not necessarily mean being liquid. Liquidity, though, is key if you are to survive and thrive as a property investor.

Profit is a key measure of success, but to achieve success you must ensure you get your cash flow management right. Many businesses go to the wall while posting apparently healthy profits all because they have not got their cash flow management right. Cash flow is essential to solvency and crucial to survival. Having money to hand will ensure loans, repairs and bills are paid on time. If you do not have enough cash to support your investment, it is likely you will run into trouble.

Forecasting is key to successful cash flow management. This is not as hard as it sounds – all you have to do is forecast what money is due in and what money is due out and when. From that you can plot your cash position to ensure you have enough to pay for your outgoings. Getting the timing of your payments right is critical. Dates should be checked of any key outgoings, such as your mortgage, to ensure you have sufficient funds. At times this can feel like a juggling act; however, the key to success lies in ensuring your payments *in* cover your payments *out* and that they are timed correctly.

Understanding your cash flow is key, especially when you plan to do any additional works, such as upgrade a kitchen. This should be planned and preferably saved for in advance. Consideration should be given to the timing of how these works may impact upon your cash flow and the anticipated uplift you hope to achieve. Projects often run over budget and schedule and this means additional costs and voids may be incurred for any overrun. Moreover, sometimes the enhanced uplift and extra money you hoped to achieve from undertaking the works may not materialise as you expected.

Having more money going out than you've got coming in can be a disastrous situation, unless you have taken the necessary action to cover it. Active cash flow management and forecasting your position are key to ensuring your cash flow remains positive and you remain in business.

Go For It!

Look at your last six months' bank statements. Choose a date of the month to plot your cash flow position from. This can be any date, but it must be the same each month. Now check and compare your balance on that date over the last six months. What has been happening to your cash flow position? Does it remain the same or move up and/or down?

Rule 55: Always have a stash of cash

You need to expect the unexpected.

No matter how carefully you plan or forecast your cash flow, unforeseen expenditure will occur. Unexpected bills will crop up, surprising issues will arise and things you thought would happen don't. Just as life will occasionally jump up and bite you in the face, so will investing in property. Tenants who have been stalwarts in paying their rent on time may suddenly lose their job, or face a relationship breakdown that means their regular payments go awry. A property can suddenly develop a fault such as a leaking roof or broken boiler, which demands a large sum of money to put right. Alternatively, a sale you thought was a 'definite' can become a 'definitely maybe' overnight and throw any hope of a profit in the near future to the far future.

To make it as a successful property investor, you need to *expect the unexpected*. Plans can quickly unravel at the best of times and it is critical you always have a back-up in mind to see you through. Having a stash of cash available to you at these times can make all the difference. It is advisable this emergency reserve fund is equivalent to at least six months' rental. This amount will usually be sufficient to cover most unexpected things and give you a back-up to see you through until the next stage.

Having a reserve fund in place not only means you will be able to pay for any unforeseen emergencies, it also acts as a mental buffer and gives you space to breathe and work out the next steps. Property investment, especially when things are going wrong, can feel an incredibly tense and fraught business. There are a huge number of interdependent parts that can start to unravel and make you feel like you are drowning. Decisions made under pressure or duress are often not the right decisions in the long run. This is why it is so important to always have a stash of cash, because this reserve fund actually gives you space and time to think properly and act accordingly in difficult situations. I have seen people often react in strange ways when they feel the 'wolf is at the door'. Avoid this situation at all costs. Build yourself a comfort zone by having a reserve fund.

Go For It!

Calculate six months' rent for your property. If you have the funds already, place them in a different bank account. If not, set up a standing order to start saving towards your reserves now. Always keep your reserve fund separate – this is a rainy day account and is not for everyday usage.

Rule 56: It's about the money, not how many

*It does not matter how many
properties you own – it only matters
how much money you make.*

As a full-time property investor, my job title is: Property Investor. And so when I meet people for the first time and I am invariably asked what I do, I reply: 'I am a property investor.' To which most people then reply: 'How many properties do you own?' And even to this day, I am astounded by this question. Not only does it show a fundamental naivety concerning the business of property investment, but it's also an incredibly private matter and not something that I tend to share as one of my opening lines. The equivalent, which many people tend to forget, would be somebody telling me they are a store manager, or whatever job they do, and me replying: 'How much do you earn?' Could you imagine the reply I would get if I asked that? My question would almost certainly be met with a frosty glare and an unprintable answer.

The fact is, when you're a property investor, your life and your business are seen as an open book by many people. They tend to forget your business is *your business* and the number of properties *you* own is a private affair. The latter is often seen by people to be a yardstick of success. If you own lots of property, you must have made it! But really, have you made it if you own thousands of properties but are mortgaged up to the eyeballs and struggling to make the mortgage payments every month? Does owning lots of properties with lots of mortgages really make you a success? I think not. Owning lots of properties *without* mortgages – now that's a different matter!

A major issue for many investors is people's obsession with the number of properties owned. There is a 'figure fascination' that underlines much thinking in the industry and it is a line of thinking that is wrong. It does not matter how many properties you own – *it only matters how much money you make*. The bottom line is actually the bottom line. There is no point owning loads of properties if you are not making any money. The only point to investing in property is to make money – if you're not, then you're not investing in property, you're just spending your money on property. It's as simple as that.

Never ever confuse owning lots of property with making lots of money. Property investment is not a race and many investors have fallen by the wayside due to their addiction to quantity over profitability.

Go For It!

Calculate how much money you earn every month and deduct your costs and expenses. The remaining figure is your disposable income – or what in the business world would be your operating profit.

Rule 57: The power of leverage

The power of leverage is that you don't just profit on the growth of your own money – you also profit on the growth of other people's money (the borrowed money).

Leverage is a powerful concept in property investment and, in simple terms, means you can use a little to get a lot. Leverage means you can use a small initial investment to buy a property that costs more money than you currently have available. Written like that, it may sound odd (and very exciting!), but that's exactly what you are doing when you take out a mortgage to buy a property: you are leveraging.

Leveraging means using other people's money (such as the bank's) to take 100 per cent control of an asset, for a fraction of the price. So think about the deposit required to buy a property – in some cases this could be as little as 5 per cent of the total price or maybe as much as 50 per cent. However, the key fact is you only had *some* of the money. You then leveraged the asset (i.e. the property) along with your deposit (i.e. some money) to raise the rest of the funds required to purchase all of it. This means that you now control the whole asset for a fraction of the price. This is leverage – and, when you leverage an asset, this makes your money go further.

So how does leverage work and why is it so powerful?

Leverage works simply because it means you can buy more than you actually have the money for. When used well, it means you can make your returns grow faster. However, the flipside is that if the market turns it also means you can lose your money faster. The key thing to remember about leverage is that it works like a magnifying glass – it *multiplies* – and this can be good and bad.

Let's look at an example of leverage in action. Let's say you have £100,000 cash. With that cash you could buy a property for £100,000 and rent it out. If the property market increased by 10 per cent in five years, the property would be worth £110,000 and you would be £10,000 better off. That is a 10 per cent return on your original investment.

However, what if you had leveraged that same cash? If you used £100,000 with a 75 per cent loan-to-value mortgage, you could buy FOUR £100,000 properties by putting down a 25 per cent deposit (£25,000) on each of them. This would then give you control of £400,000 worth of assets. This is a four-fold increase on the same amount of money when leverage is added. If the property market increased by 10 per cent in five years, the properties would be worth £440,000 and you would be £40,000 better off. That is a 40 per cent return on your original investment.

The power of leverage is that you don't just profit on the growth of your own money – you also profit on the growth of *other people's money* (the borrowed money).

Of course, if the market drops, your losses are also multiplied. For example, if the property market fell by 10 per cent, your original cash purchase property of £100,000 would now be worth £90,000 and you would have lost £10,000 of your original investment (10 per cent). However, your £400,000 of leveraged properties would now only be worth £360,000, meaning you would have lost £40,000 of your original investment (40 per cent).

The power of leverage really comes into its own when a property has been bought with sufficient rental income to cover the cost of the leverage (interest on the loan) every month and the running costs (remember, more properties mean more maintenance). This allows you not only to profit from the monthly cash flow of the property, but also to retain control of the asset and enjoy any future capital appreciation with nothing more to pay than the initial deposit.

Go For It!

Check out the current mortgage deals and look at the loans-to-value percentage – this is leveraging. Now calculate what you can buy if you were to leverage your funds with a mortgage.

Rule 58: Always make an income

Income is required to pay for the day-to-day running costs of the portfolio, and hopefully, in time, your everyday living expenses.

The property market moves in cycles. Up. Down. Up. Down. And at this point I could throw in the much over-used saying about how property values double every seven to ten years, but I won't. I think the past few years of endemic turmoil have taught us that we are entering uncharted territory. What property prices will do now is anybody's guess. Commentators across the globe talk of upswings, gains, bubbles and the like, while others sit bewailing the loss of value. Lending levels are increasing, and yet simultaneously lenders are imposing tighter criteria. More people are buying, and yet less people are selling. More people are in debt, and yet less people are spending. Inconsistency is about the only thing that is consistent in the current property reports.

However, property that is bought on the fundamentals of making an income is less exposed to the vagaries of the market. If property has been bought to produce an income – regardless of its capital value – what the market is doing will have little to no impact, as long as the asset is producing an income. Buying for income is a simplistic idea, but it is often overlooked by investors as they seek the starry returns of capital growth. Buying for income is not sexy, nor will it make you a millionaire overnight, but it will put money into your pocket every month of the year. Income-producing properties are reliable and consistent. They may not dramatically increase in value, but they are solid earners and will produce regular cash flow, which is what you need to live on.

Property needs to be treated as a business asset and, to that end, the income an asset produces should be calculated carefully and understood as a business investment. Capital appreciation, while able to produce stellar results, can only be leveraged when an asset is borrowed against or sold. Income is required to pay for the day-to-day running costs of the portfolio, and hopefully, in time, your everyday living expenses. This is why it is essential you understand the rental yields and ensure your investment produces an income. Creating multiple income streams and making workhorses of certain property investments will ensure you have sufficient cash flow that can buffer and protect your assets from the roller-coaster ride of the property market. Do this well and you will soon be on your way to ditching the day job!

Go For It!

Calculate your own personal budget and work out how much income you need to ditch the day job.

Rule 59: You need to calculate to accumulate

It is critical to understand if the reward is worth the risk – and if you can cope with the risk if the rewards don't pay out.

You often hear the phrase 'You have to speculate to accumulate' when it comes to property investment. But I think this line of thinking verges on an unnecessarily risky mentality, and believe the phrase *you need to calculate to accumulate* is a more appropriate attitude to investment.

To accumulate you need to calculate. And, when it comes to property, that means doing your market research and negotiating a deal that stacks. People who have lost money in property are usually those who 'speculated' without calculating. They bought without conducting the necessary research and speculated on the future value of the asset. Many investors who piled into new-build, off-plan and areas they didn't know, got caught in the speculation-without-calculation trap. Property values can fall as well as rise.

Speculation *can* lead to accumulation – but it must be calculated. Speculating on gaining planning permission for a piece of land or redeveloping a site can lead to big wins. But understanding the risk-to-reward ratio of your purchase is critical to knowing if a risk is worth taking – and if you can afford to take it. In any speculative purchase, calculations need to be carried out: you need to assess what you plan to gain, and what you stand to lose. It is critical to understand if the reward is worth the risk – and whether you can cope with the risk if the rewards don't pay out. 'Hope value' needs to be quantified and 'risks' need to be reckoned. Even if you don't have all the answers, you need to plan for the worst- and best-case scenario.

Speculation requires resources and it is important to assess if those means could be channelled into other opportunities. Every project has an opportunity cost attached to it – that is, the opportunity of doing a different project that could deliver different or better results. Resources are not just about time and money – they are also about the energy, hassle and headspace that different projects will demand of you. These should always be factored into any plan as not all projects are equal!

Successful speculation requires careful calculation. You should always be clear of the risks you are taking and only gamble what you are prepared, or able, to lose. Speculation is not the same as investment. Speculators hope for the best, investors know the best.

Go For It!

Calculate your 'speculation' threshold. What reward would you want in return for risking your savings and six months of your life?

Rule 60: Get to grips with gross and net yields

*Gross rental yields are those calculated before **deductions have been made.** Net rental yields are those calculated after **deductions have been made.***

When you invest in property, the return you receive is called a yield. There are two yields calculated – one is the rental yield and this is related to the income you receive from the property. The other is called the capital growth yield, and this is derived from the capital value of the property (the calculation for this is in Rule 62: You can't have it all). If you are looking to hold a property for the long term and produce an income, it is essential you understand the rental yield of a property. You will often hear people talk about gross and net rental yields – there is a major difference between the two: gross rental yields are those calculated *before* deductions; net rental yields are those calculated *after* deductions have been made. This is like the equivalent of your gross salary and your net salary – and, as you will be aware, there is a major difference between the two!

Calculating gross yields can be a useful comparison tool when you want to assess a property quickly. This is how you calculate gross rental yield:

(Annual rent/purchase price) × 100 = gross rental yield.

Thus, if a property was purchased for £100,000 and the rental income was £600 per month, this is how you would calculate the gross rental yield:

(£7,200 [annual rent] / £100,000 [purchase price]) × 100 = 7.2% [gross rental yield].

To calculate the net yield, you need to include all costs associated with buying the property, including any ongoing maintenance works, insurance, void periods, etc.

Thus, for example, in the net yield calculation we would need to add purchase costs to the £100,000 property purchase price:

Mortgage arrangement fee:	£999
Solicitor's costs:	£750
Survey fee:	£250
Maintenance/renovation:	£2,500
Sub-total:	**£4,499**
Grand Total:	**£104,499**

In addition to the extra purchase costs, to obtain a net yield calculation, you also need to include the running costs of the property. A good rule of thumb is to allow a vacancy of one month per year and 10 per cent of the annual rent for ongoing maintenance, repairs and insurance.

To continue with the above example, the figures would include:

Annual rent:	£7,200
	(£600 per month × 12)
Minus one month void per year:	£600
Minus 10 per cent of annual rent for ongoing maintenance:	£720
Total Net Annual Income:	**£5,880**

To calculate the net yields, the figures for both the purchase price and net annual income would be used.

Using the above example, the net yield calculation looks as follows:

(£5,880 [annual rent – running costs] / £104,499 [property & costs]) × 100 = 5.6% [net rental yield].

While these calculations show you how to obtain a net rental yield, they do not allow for other items such as agency fees and tax and these should be factored in according to your personal circumstances. These figures also do not include capital appreciation, which can vary according to the property purchased.

Go For It!

Using the calculations provided, work through your own property example to calculate the net yields.

Rule 61: Run the numbers before you invest

Not every property will make money and some will perform better than others.

With so many properties available to invest in, you need to ensure you are making the most of what you've got. The best way to do that is to run the numbers and calculate how different properties compare. Not every property will make money and some will perform better than others. There are a variety of different calculations that can be used; however, I stick to three simple ratios: Net Annual Yield (the calculation for this is in Rule 60); Return on Investment (ROI); and Cash Margin.

When running the numbers, a good rule of thumb is to allow a vacancy of one month per year and 10 per cent of the annual rent for ongoing maintenance, repairs and insurance. You will also need to include any additional refurbishment expenses or agency fees, as required.

The illustration below is a worked example of a £100,000 property, bought with a 75 per cent mortgage and a monthly rental of £600 per month. The costs are approximate.

How to run the numbers:

Start with the purchase of the property:

- Purchase price: £100,000
- Mortgage: £75,000
  (75 per cent loan to value, 25-year
  mortgage at 5 per cent interest)
- Purchase costs: £2,000
- Renovation costs: £1,000

From the above figures you can calculate the Total Cash Invested (TCI):

- Total Cash   = Purchase Price – Mortgage + Purchase Costs +
  Invested (TCI)   Renovation Costs

- TCI = £100,000 – £75,000 + £2,000 + £1,000 = £28,000

Now you need to calculate the Monthly Cash Flow (MCF):

- Monthly Cash Flow = Monthly Income – Monthly Expenses.

Using the example above, the figures would include:

- Rental income (PCM):   £600 per month
  Minus monthly expenses:
- Mortgage interest: £312.50 per month
                              (£75,000 × 5% interest/12)
- Void allowance: £50 per month (£600/12 months)
- Maintenance allowance: £60 per month (10% of rent)
- MCF =   £600 (monthly income) –
                              £422.50 (monthly costs) = £177.50

Using the above example, this shows you have a Monthly Cash Flow of £177.50 per month. This is the surplus cash you will be making each month after taking into account the estimated expenses.

By running these numbers, you can now calculate the key ratios to indicate how the property will perform as an investment:

Return on Investment (ROI)

ROI = Monthly Cash Flow × 12 Months / Total Cash Invested

(£177.50 × 12 / £28,000) × 100 = 7.60%

The ROI shows the annual return on the cash invested in a property.

Cash Margin

Cash Margin = Monthly Cash Flow / Monthly Income

(£177.50 / £600) × 100 = 29.58%

A Cash Margin of 29.58 per cent means you get to keep, on average, just under one-third of the rent you collect after costs. Cash Margins are very useful ratios when comparing properties – the higher the margin, the more money there is to be made and the better buffer you have if rents fall or costs increase.

These performance ratios mean you can compare properties to see which give you the best rental returns. ROIs should be assessed against the risk, effort, time and money involved. It is important to remember these figures do not allow for any capital appreciation, nor do they include the repayment of the mortgage, tax or agency fees, which should be included according to your individual circumstances.

Go For It!

Choose two property deals you have seen. Run the numbers on both properties and see how they stack up. Compare the two properties and understand how each performs.

Rule 62: You can't have it all

Properties that achieve the highest
rental yields have the least chance of
capital growth yield and vice versa.

To a certain degree, property investment can offer the best of both worlds: it's possible to earn an income from an asset and for the underlying value of the asset to appreciate over time. However, having said that, there is usually an inverse correlation between the rental yield and the capital growth yield. That is, properties that achieve the highest rental yields have the least chance of capital growth yield and vice versa. This means some properties will perform better on rental yields, while others will perform better on capital growth. This means, unfortunately, you *can't* have it all.

From the outset, and as part of your investment objectives, you need to decide what you want and/or need more: income or capital. Deciding which of these is more important to you will dictate the type of properties you buy. This will mean, if you are targeting capital growth properties, you will likely be buying in more expensive areas and will need to put down a larger equity stake to ensure you meet the rental ratio set by many mortgage lenders. (This is usually 125 per cent of the interest payment. That means that if the mortgage interest payment is £100 per month, the lender will require your rent to be £125: 125 per cent of the interest payment). However, if you want income from day one to ditch the day job, then you will be looking for higher rental yields against a lower capital outlay. These properties will tend to be cheaper and not in such salubrious areas – however, they will probably make surplus money every month for you to bank.

One of the beauties of running a property investment business is the number of costs that can be offset against tax. The most valuable tax deduction is the mortgage interest that can be offset against the rental received. Moreover, there are opportunities to offset repairs and improvements to the property as either revenue or capital expenses. This is not to mention the agency fees that can be deducted and any expenses you have incurred as a result of running the business. This makes property investment a very tax-efficient use of funds. However, it must be noted there is a clear distinction between capital and revenue expenses and how these are set off, and you should discuss these with a professional tax advisor.

Capital growth yields are calculated differently to rental yields. Capital growth is the price appreciation on an investment relative to the amount that was initially invested. For example, if a property was bought for £100,000 and the value increases to £150,000, the capital growth yield is 50 per cent. It is calculated as follows:

Capital growth yield =

(market price of a property – original purchase price) / original purchase price × 100.

Thus, the worked example would look like this:

(£150,000 – £100,000) / £100,000 × 100 = 50%.

Capital growth yields can be notoriously difficult to predict and the value of a property can go down as well as up.

Capital growth yields and rental yields are completely different animals with very different outcomes. This means you need to plan from the beginning if you want to make regular amounts of money, or you want a big payoff in the future. Of course, the trick to having it all could be to opt for a 'blended approach' – that is, you buy properties with high rental yields to support the properties bought for capital growth potential.

Go For It!

Calculate the capital growth yields of a property by analysing land registry prices over the last ten years. This information can be obtained by putting your postcode into websites such as www.nethouseprices.com. Work out the capital growth of a property by analysing the prices over the years and how these have changed. This will show you the capital growth potential of the area.

Rule 63: Re-mortgaging is not free recycling

Re-mortgaging means you can cash in on the 'profit' of a property, without actually having to sell the property.

There is a commonly held belief that re-mortgaging a property to withdraw the equity is recycling your money, but re-mortgaging is not *free* recycling. Re-mortgaging is increasing your debt levels. Yes, you may be pulling your money out of a deal, but you'll be replacing it with the bank's instead. Re-mortgaging to withdraw equity will give you real money to spend and the ability to increase your portfolio, but it is not *free* money. It is not the same as selling a property and cashing in on the real value increase with cold, hard cash.

Re-mortgaging means you can cash in on the equity of a property, without actually having to sell. To this end, re-mortgaging is like taking a 'paper profit' – that is, *on paper* the property appears to have increased in value, and so by re-mortgaging you are taking that increase in value without having to dispose of the asset. This strategy can work well in a rising market, where you have undertaken works to increase the capital value of a property, or bought particularly below market value. However, it should always be remembered that re-mortgaging is only taking a 'paper profit' – it is not the 'real profit' that you would gain if somebody bought your property. The re-valuation figure is *not* the same as the market value for the property. One is for the purposes of a new bank loan (the re-mortgage); the other is the actual real money people would give you to buy your property – they are two different things.

The beauty of re-mortgaging and the reason why it is so popular is its flexibility: you can get real money out of your property without having to sell it. The flipside – which so many people conveniently tend to forget – is this is *real* debt. By re-mortgaging and withdrawing equity, you have increased the loan secured against the property and the amount of debt and interest owed. Moreover, the 'paper profit' you have taken also creates a future tax liability when you eventually sell the property. These factors should always be taken into consideration.

Re-mortgaging is also expensive and will likely incur costs from solicitors and surveyors, not to mention additional arrangement fees. While many of the charges can be added to the mortgage, it is important to calculate the *true cost* of re-mortgaging to ensure the cost of withdrawing the equity makes financial sense. When all of the costs are added together, it can be surprising how much a re-mortgage costs!

It is wise to re-mortgage with care and make sure your 'recycled' funds are worth the fees and the additional debt you are taking on. Understand leverage can also work against you. Read the small print, check your mortgage is suitable, and don't make debt a default – at some point it will need paying back.

Go For It!

Analyse the true cost of a re-mortgage by adding together all the fees and expenses you will incur, along with the increased interest payments. Include the arrangement fee, redemption fee, solicitor fee, broker fee, surveyor fee, etc., and be very clear about the cost implication of drawing a 'paper profit'.

Rule 64: The grass isn't always greener

The problem with eye-balling other people's stuff is it means you take your own eye off the ball.

Human nature means we're inherently thinking other people have got it easier, better and anything else *–er* than us. Frankly, whatever we've got, it always seems like someone else has got more. And we get jealous. We want more; more of what they've got – and a little bit extra for good measure. And yet, when we get more, we will always find someone else who has something *more* – something that outshines and surpasses what we thought we wanted and would be happy with.

The grass always looks greener on the other side. This side of the fence, that is *your* side of the fence, is never as lustrous, or as glossy as the other side. The other side always seems to have more. And you're always left wanting and yearning for that something extra.

It's high time you get to grips with this 'more' mentality and understand that, no matter what you do, somebody will always have more. Even if you make it to a gazillion properties, somebody will always have a gazillion and one. It's an ongoing race with other people to try to get more and more, and more and more. Maybe you'll be on top for a bit, but then what? Unless you keep racing to win, somebody will beat you – they will have more. Then you'll have less and you'll be back where you started.

And the thing is, all this racing to win and trying to go one better means you don't even feel grateful or happy for what you have, or what you've achieved. When you keep thinking you should do *more*, everything you have is tinged with a 'less than' quality; it's never quite good enough. This leads not only to unhappiness but also to an infatuation with other people, and other people's business.

The problem with eye-balling other people's stuff is it means you take your own eye off the ball. It means you don't care for your side of the fence quite as well as you should. You end up *not* focusing on what it is you should be doing. When you're so worried about what everybody else is doing or having, it doesn't leave much room for you to concentrate on you and what you should be doing.

So my advice to you is this: be happy with what you're doing and make the most of what you've got. Plan your success, know your path, strive to win – but don't compete for the sake of competition. Enjoy being a player and participating in the market. The grass is not always greener – we just think it is.

Go For It!

Write down a list of people who have more than you – it can be anything you feel they have more of; for example, money, time, confidence, etc. Be honest with yourself – what do you really want *more* of in your life? What *more* would really make the difference to you?

Rule 65: Get used to coming second best

*If you want to succeed,
your business comes first
and you come second.*

Building a money-making property business does not happen overnight. There is no get-rich-quick. Yes, some people get lucky – gambles can pay off, markets can meteorically rise – but, on an everyday basis, success needs to be planned. Getting a business off the ground can be a hard slog – it takes time, effort and money to build it. And there will be moments when you wonder: is it worth it? When you are in the early stages of building your business, you have to focus on the future outcome – the good times that will come as a result of your efforts now. That means putting the needs of the business first. It's rather like having children – the business needs to be your priority if it is to grow into a stable and well-adjusted adult. But what you need to keep in mind is the future payback of property investment: look after a property well, and it will look after you well.

What, though, does being second best mean? It means, unfortunately, sometimes going without. It means your being a lower priority than your business. It means your tenants' needs come above your own needs. It means doing everything in your power to ensure your business survives and thrives. It means what it says on the tin: you are second best. And that can be tough in the beginning. It can feel like everything you do and all your resources are spent on building your property business. But, if you want to really succeed, your business comes first and you come second.

Now this all may sound very depressing and boring, and you may even be questioning *why* you want to get into property investment, or in fact why you *have* invested. But let me tell you: it's for the long term. You are playing the long game. Owning and running a property business may be hard work in the beginning, and it may feel like a never-ending drain on your resources, but look after it right and *it will look after you right*.

Be patient. Run your business to the best of your ability and understand that making money takes time. Once you have perfected the art of looking after your business interests, you will learn what this actually means is looking after your *own* best interests. By knowing this, you will feel a lot less frustrated by what you are missing, because of what you stand to gain in the future. And the sacrifices you make now will be worth much, much more when you come to collect your winnings in the future.

Go For It!

Look at one of your prized possessions. How much do you value it? Would you be prepared to sell it to keep your business going? If not, think carefully before you invest in property because sometimes you will have to make personal sacrifices.

Rule 66: Keep squeaky clean

Showing you respect the rules of
credit protects your credit line.

There is one fundamental Rule to remember about getting credit: banks only like to lend to people who *don't* really need to borrow. That means you always need to show yourself to be a trusted person when it comes to handling credit. How you manage credit (and let's be honest, this is actually debt) shows banks, companies and lenders what sort of person you are. People who pay their credit on time and in full get more credit. Credit begets credit. It's a simple virtuous circle – the more credit you can handle, the more credit you can raise.

However, a cardinal Rule should not be overlooked: never ever use up *all* your credit. Using up all your credit (even if you are allowed to) looks bad. Companies don't like people who take *too* much credit. Having access to it is one thing – but using it all up, that's a different kettle of fish! It may be that you have several credit cards each with a £10,000 limit – but that is not to say you should use them. Maxing out credit lines is a 'no-no'. Someone who has used up all their credit will struggle to find *more* credit. Having too much 'used credit' makes people nervous; nobody wants to be at the end of the queue when they're owed money.

Paying bills is a necessary evil – and paying them on time and as demanded is the only way to ensure you keep your credit record clean. Remember, your record is the only way you are going to secure more credit in the future – when it comes to raising finance, your credit history is your future. That means you must have a system in place to ensure everything is paid as it should be. With life being so busy it's easy for bills to slip through the net – but late payments show up. Late payments and unpaid bills leave a footprint on your record; they dirty your record and make it difficult to obtain more credit in the future. All bills should be paid by direct debit to avoid any forgetfulness or oversights – credit records do not understand 'I forgot' or 'my dog ate the cheque'.

Showing you respect the Rules of credit protects your credit line. And, unless you have a major wad of cash to hand, you're going to need credit to invest in property. The only way to raise credit is to show what a squeaky clean borrower you are. Banks and lenders don't like taking risks – they want to know the money they lend is going to be paid back. The only proof you have of this is your credit record, which is why you need to keep it squeaky clean.

Hard times do happen. Sometimes finances get stretched and squeezed to within an inch of their life. However, if you are on top of your cash flow forecast, you will have seen this coming. Early and clear communication is the best way to manage creditors. Mortgages, secured loans, council tax and utility bills should all take priority. Payment plans should be negotiated ahead of time and an action plan formulated. Keeping clean won't keep you out of trouble all the time, but if you do face difficulties you'll at least have built up a reliable history to fall back on.

Go For It!

Obtain a free copy of your credit report from Experian or Equifax to see how lenders view your credit-worthiness.

Rule 67: Do sweat the small stuff

The devil really is in the detail.

Faced with decisions about what property to buy, where, how much to spend, and so forth can leave you thinking property investment is all about making BIG decisions. But actually, some of the big decisions are the easiest. Once you've decided the sort of property you want to buy, your budget, the location and all the rest of that malarkey, the hard part is then the detail. And, like the saying goes – the devil really is in the detail. Yes, I know you may be very busy while planning to be an incredibly rich and successful property investor, but small details matter. And I'm not just talking about whether or not to opt for satin-finish light switches!

In the big decision-making period of property investment, it's easy to forget about the little things, the not-so-important things, the things-that-can-be-left-to-another-day things. Well, I'm here to correct you. *Little things matter.* Small stuff can easily turn into *big* stuff unless you deal with it promptly and efficiently. So all the *little* things you've been meaning to do, or have been putting off for another day – do them.

Inform the council tax department you are the new owner, take the meter readings and let the utility suppliers know, change the locks on the doors, introduce yourself to the new neighbours, check that the insurance policy you have is adequate (especially if you are doing work to the property), take the time to read the contracts from the letting/sales agents, check the small print and make sure you know what you're signing, set up direct debits with any suppliers to avoid late payments, call the roofer to fix that slipped tile, find the EPC from the property file, organise the Gas Safe certificate, check all furniture is fire safe, make sure you have detailed inventories, note down any paint used for future reference, and so on and so forth.

Details, details, details – they can be such an absolute pain and a thief of time. But, if you don't do the small stuff now, it grows into big stuff in the end. Take, for example, that paint colour that you knew you would remember when you needed to buy it again so you didn't bother to write it down because you were so busy doing something *far* more important. Two years later and you just can't remember the colour for the life of you. You were pretty sure it was some sort of Magnolia-type colour – but from what store and what exact shade? Noting down this minor detail at the outset would have meant that two years later you're not running around chasing your tail and trying to work out the shade of paint you bought. Don't believe me? Well, you'll be redecorating the entire property rather than just touching up bits unless you can track down the exact match! The devil really is in the detail, and in making sure small stuff gets done. If it doesn't, in time, you will painfully learn how very easy it is to make a mountain out of what should have been a molehill.

Go For It!

Write a to-do list of all the mundane 'little' things you need to do. When your energy levels are low, or you have a few minutes to spare, plug the time gaps in your day with items from the list.

Rule 68: Problems are like buses

*Problems are just questions waiting
for solutions.*

I've got to give you this warning now, before you jump in with both feet. Sometimes things can get hairy and incredibly scary and you will feel like you are drowning – as though nothing else can hit the fan. You're beat and you're spent. But let me tell you something – those times will pass. The fan will work again, the stuff goes away and then it's back on to another day.

Problems, when they arise, don't often come in ones. Like buses, they don't show up for ages at a time, and then they all come at once when you least expect them. You can go for weeks, if not months, with everything feeling like its plain sailing and you can't believe you're even making money from what you're doing. Then something will happen. It will usually be something big and expensive, and it will remind you of the risks involved in property investment. This is par for the course. It is normal and to be expected. This is all part of the roller-coaster ride of property investment.

What I have to tell you is this: *do not panic*. At the time when everything is happening all at once and you hardly have time to breathe, let alone think, please don't panic. Just remember, this is the normal course of events. It will work itself out, you will come out the other side and things will go back to plain sailing once more.

Problems happen. This is just a fact of life and a fact of business. It's how you face and deal with them that matters. Never ever put your head in the sand: you cannot see what is happening. You probably won't want to see what's happening, of course, nor feel you have the strength to deal with it. But you will and you can. It's called 'reserve energy'. You shouldn't use it too much, as it's really only a back-up to get through the bad times. But it will be there when you need it most, much like those reserve amounts of cash you need for when things happen, or that back-up plumber when your regular guy has let you down.

Back-ups, and remembering there is always a back-up, is what you need to do when problems arise. The heating has stopped working and you can't find a plumber for love nor money? Tell the tenant to go and buy some electric heaters and send them the money via internet banking to cover the cost, or call the shop yourself and pay by credit card over the phone. In the meantime, they'll have to boil the kettle for hot water and shower at the neighbours or the local gym. Tell them you'll credit them some rent for the inconvenience. Then call a local letting agency and ask them for a recommendation for a plumber. Call enough of them and you'll find a plumber to attend. Problems are just questions waiting for solutions. Your role is to juggle the questions until you find the right answers. In the meantime, just keep plate-spinning in the assurance that this time will pass. Soon enough, everything will be plain sailing again.

Go For It!

Get a back-up plan in place. If you only know one plumber, act now to get to know a few more – same goes for an electrician, a handyman and a locksmith. Knowing who to call if your first-choice tradesperson is not available gives you options and alternatives.

Rule 69: Know your competition

*There is no excuse for not knowing
what your competition is doing.*

With so many properties out there for people to choose from, what is it about yours that will make them choose it? If you've abided by the Rule to Buy something special (Rule 41), you're at least in with half a chance – you'll have something different to offer to the market. But do you know the market? Do you know what your competition is doing? Being aware of what is happening in the marketplace is critical if you are to stay ahead. Tastes change, areas go in and out of fashion, prices fluctuate – the property market is a moving feast. The playing field is not level – different players are entering all the time and are changing and breaking the rules.

There is no excuse for not knowing what your competition is doing. It takes just a few minutes' research online. Property portals such as Rightmove and Zoopla show you what your competition is doing in a flash. Knowing what is happening in your area needs to become second nature – you need to be familiar with what is for sale and rent and at what price, at any given time. Set up search alerts so that you are notified every time a new property is added to the site within your area. Watch what properties are being added and look at the internal designs and the price they are asking.

Monitor new additions and check how long it takes to sell/rent the property. Both Zoopla and Rightmove display the date the property was first listed – check regularly for any updates to the status. If a property sold or rented particularly fast, call the agent. Ask them why the property went so fast – what was it that people liked so much? Write it down and keep it for future reference. If a property you're monitoring is sticking, call the agents. Ask them about the property and find out why it's not moving. Understand what the issues and barriers are in the marketplace and think about how these may apply to your property, if at all.

View the competition. If you have a property for sale or rent, go and see other properties that you think are comparable to yours. Don't be afraid to know what you're up against. View them, assess them, go back to your property and see what you can do better. What can you do differently? What do you need to change to make your property the top choice for people? Perhaps you need to lower the price, redecorate, change the kitchen or simply just dress it better? These are all ideas that, until you know what your competition is doing, you'll just be guessing at.

Ask for honest feedback. Understand exactly what it is people think of your property. Know what you have done right and what you have done wrong. Look to put things right. Change what you need to change to get the result you want. Remember you are in competition with other properties and other people – this is not a one-horse race. Know who you are up against and do what you need to win.

Go For It!

Go on Rightmove and Zoopla and enter the postcode of your property. Search for properties for sale and rent within a quarter-mile and half-mile radius. Check the properties and assess them against yours. How does yours compare with the competition?

Rule 70: Keep your finger on the pulse

To remain competitive and in demand you need to keep up to date with the changing marketplace around you.

The property market is dynamic and, to remain competitive and in demand, you need to keep up to date with the changing marketplace around you. It is advisable to regularly do comparison research online as it can be valuable in identifying any emerging patterns in the property market.

The key insights to be gleaned are:

- **Strength of the market:** By checking the number of properties available on the market and the listing dates on Rightmove and Zoopla, you can assess how much stock is available and how long it takes to sell and/or rent in the area. Local agents should also be called to discuss current demand and supply levels, plus timings for completions.

- **Décor and interior trends:** By looking at comparable properties you will notice various styles of presentation. Any particular looks or themes that appear to be on trend, such as changes to layout, garden design and so forth, should be noted. These can be further assessed for their popularity and potential to add value.

- **Local developments:** Lettings and estate agents are a rich source of local knowledge when it comes to new property developments. While talking with them, you should take the opportunity to discuss any new or planned developments, and what impact these may have on the market.

- **Market dynamics:** Checking comparable properties is a good indicator of the changing dynamics in the marketplace. For example, it may be possible to identify a new breed of customer entering the market if you notice an increase in designer-labelled kitchen appliances or sanitary ware.

- **Structural changes:** Property details can be a gold-mine of information; look out for any buzzwords that agents use, such as proximity to new developments and changes in the local area. Talk to agents about any new planned improvements (e.g. new retailers opening, transport links, employers). Be mindful of any large-scale company closures that may impact upon customer demand in your area.

By understanding the key trends and changes in the local market, you will be better placed to take action where necessary and, in some cases, to adapt your strategy to fit with changing needs. Keeping in touch with the market will enable you to anticipate and plan for developments you may need to make within your business. It will also provide insight into areas where additional value can be added. By comparing your property to the competition, you can ensure it's performing at its best – and, if not, take the required action to make sure it is!

Go For It!

Search for property ads in your local area and look at the photographs carefully. What design trends do you see? Are there any particular styles you like or don't like? What improvements could you make to your property to make sure you remain competitive?

Rule 71: Build a dream team

*Don't be afraid to use people who
know more than you – actively
seek out people who are more
knowledgeable and learn from them.*

I have often seen people fall into the trap of what I call 'island thinking'; that is, they think of themselves as an island. They try to do as much as they can themselves in their property business for fear of being ripped off or screwed over by other people. I can truly understand this; trust is difficult to give. But, to get on in this business, you need to build bridges from your island to connect with other people. Of course, you should always be mindful of the Rules of who you do business with, but you *do* need to do business with others. Business makes the world go round, and it will help yours go round quicker and easier once you have a dream team in place.

So what are the components of a dream team? To start with, you need to find the source of your business. This may be an estate agent you have managed to befriend, an auction house or maybe even a property sourcer. The key point is that they need to be able to supply you with deals or leads that will help you to buy properties. The second part of the equation is to find a trusted agent or person to look after your property. Even if you plan to manage the property yourself, it's likely you will need some assistance in the future, so find your dream-team member now. The same is true when selling – having a trusted person you can call upon makes all the difference to achieving a sale.

You need to find a broker or bank manager you can talk to and who believes in you. Finding and raising finance can be extremely time-consuming and difficult. By working with professionals in the industry and setting forward your business case, you are in a better position to take advantage of deals when they come along. Think like a business, show your financial workings, display how you intend to make money and show how you have arrived at your calculations. People want to help people who help themselves – help yourself by showing what a strong business case you have.

Find a friendly and down-to-earth solicitor who speaks in plain English and doesn't try to bamboozle you with legalese. Feel comfortable asking questions and understand the ins and outs of any deals. Good solicitors can provide a wealth of information and have unique access and insight to the property market, which can enable you to make better decisions. If you are planning to rent your property, it is a good idea to have a solicitor on hand for advice, should the need ever arise.

A great builder, able to turn his or her hand to most projects or at least advise on what is entailed, is a key part of your dream team. Look to build long-term trusted working partnerships where you are able to call on him/her for small and/or big jobs. Be fair in your dealings and understand that tradespeople also need to earn a living. Professionals don't like to cut corners, so try to avoid putting them in a position where they will not feel proud of their work.

Aim to build a dream team that is better than you. Don't

be afraid to use people who know more than you – actively seek out those who are more knowledgeable and learn from them. Set your standards high and aim to measure up to them yourself.

Go For It!

Begin putting together your dream team. Ask friends, family and colleagues for recommendations and start to locate the key members you want to do business with.

Rule 72: Only do business with people you like

People like doing business with people they like.

I know it may sound a stretch to only do business with people you like – but I reckon, even if you can't manage it *all* the time, you should at least try to aim for it *most* of the time. Now that you're your own boss, if you can't choose who you want to do business with, then when can you? The fact of the matter is that people like doing business with people they like. And the more you like people, the better business you will do. So it makes sense, really, to only do business with people you like.

But how can you work out if you like people? Everybody has their own methods, but for me I have an easy litmus test to help me decide – I call it the 'pub test'. In essence, I ask myself: 'Would I like to spend an evening down the pub with you?' I think to myself: 'Would we have anything to talk about? What other interests might we share outside of property? Would I actually enjoy spending time in your company?' It doesn't necessarily mean I intend to spend an evening down the pub, but simply asking such questions helps me to recognise whether or not I've found the sort of person with whom I want to do business.

You will have your own ways to decide whether you like someone and want to do business with them, but the key thing to remember is that it is *your* choice. Business relationships are *chosen*. The more successful ones are chosen because they benefit both parties and are built on mutual respect. This means they are more likely to last longer, and in business long-term and trusted relationships are key to building future, sustainable success.

Over time, issues and challenges will arise that will test the strength of any business relationship, and these can make or break them. People respond to situations in different ways, and you will learn much about them through their response. In my experience, working with people you like, at such times, makes things easier. Having a personal connection in place means that everybody tends to pull together, work harder and strive to find solutions to problems more swiftly.

Go For It!

Write down a list of the companies/people you like doing business with, and another of those you do *not* like doing business with. Make a note of how often you contact those in the first (like) list compared with those in the second (dislike) list.

Rule 73: Be careful who you get into bed with

Choosing a joint venture partner should be approached in the same way as choosing a business partner.

Joint ventures can be a great way to get the most out of what you've got. By combining resources with someone, you may be able to trade up and buy a better property than you could on your own, or you may need less money to get started in the first place. This arrangement can work wonders when you get on with your partner(s) and share the same aims and outcomes for the project. To get the most out of any joint venture, it is best practice to write up a financial plan with time-orientated goals and have an agreement in place from the outset.

Joint ventures can take many forms and how they are structured depends on an individual's requirements. It may be that two people join together to buy a property fifty/fifty (each party contributing an equal amount of money), or it may be that one party does not have the same level of funds, but has more time or skills to add to the deal. Again, this can be structured as a joint venture, with the agreement taking into account the different skills and funds that each party is bringing to the deal.

Choosing a joint venture partner should be approached in the same way as choosing a business partner. Property investment is a business and your joint venture partner will become, in effect, your business partner. Even if you get together with the aim of refurbishing properties for sale, it is important to think ahead to what you would do if a property failed to sell, or if you needed to hold on to it for longer than anticipated. Thus, any joint ventures should be approached with a longer-term commitment in mind. This means you should conduct due diligence on your proposed partner, including credit checks, to ensure they can commit to the investment in the long run. This will ensure the best interests of the property are protected and gives you security in the partnership. Moreover, if the partnership is successful, you'll be hoping to do business together for many years to come!

Getting it all in writing from the outset means that all parties are clear on the outcomes of the property. The document should detail what to do if disagreements develop or the partnership is dissolved. It is best practice to set up a separate bank account solely for the property, requiring both signatories to withdraw funds. This account should be credited with a minimum amount equivalent to at least six months' rental, to cover any voids and repairs. The rental income should be paid into this account and any expenses, such as the mortgage, should be withdrawn from this. This will mean the property is better protected in the long term and no confusion of individual finances can occur.

Go For It!

Make a list of your family and friends. Are any of them suitable candidates to be joint venture partners?

Rule 74: Be sure of who you're doing business with

Doing your homework is critical.
That means undertaking research on
anybody with whom you intend to
do business.

Property investment requires you to do business with a variety of different parties. Even if you try to do much of it yourself, and don't need a mortgage, you will be surprised at the number of different people on whom you will need to rely to get things done. All of these people will, in effect, create a chain of interdependencies. This can have beneficial outcomes, but you need to be sure of those you're doing business with.

Doing your homework is critical. That means undertaking research on anybody with whom you intend to do business, be they solicitors, agents, tenants, builders and so on. Recommendations should always be sought as a first port of call, but they should not be relied on entirely. It takes just a few minutes to input a name into Google to check out the person or company further. Any reviews that people have written should be read and analysed, especially if they are from an independent website rather than a company's own testimonials page. Nowadays, it is very hard to live off the 'Google radar' and most people and companies will have some form of internet presence. In fact, if they are not to be found on the internet, your next question should be: *why?*

If you are intending to spend a considerable amount of money with a supplier or having to place trust in a company, it is advisable to do a search on Companies House. The details held should correspond with any you have been given – if they are different, you should ask why. Also, it is best practice to conduct a credit check on any companies that you plan to do business with. This is similar to conducting a tenant reference check and will give you a good understanding of the company's trading activities. This may sound a little OTT; however, many agents go bankrupt, along with architect firms and even solicitors.

Many companies go to great lengths to become professionally accredited, and join member organisations to give customers reassurance concerning the service and/or product they are selling. These professional qualifications are often taken at face value by customers when they see a logo or badge displayed. However, it is advisable to double-check any qualifications, accreditations or membership claims with the registering or authorising body. This can often be done online or by calling the organisation directly. For example, an agent who claims to be a member of the Property Ombudsman and who displays their logo should have their credentials checked with the Property Ombudsman to ensure that they are, in fact, members. It is not unknown for agents to claim to be members of a scheme when they are not – worse still, some agents may even have had their membership revoked. Facts should always be checked, rather than being taken at face value.

Go For It!

Visit the Gas Safe website (www.gassaferegister.co.uk/), enter the details of a plumber and check if they are registered with the authorising body.

Rule 75: Know when to walk away

Success is about choosing what to stop doing, as much as it is about choosing what to start doing.

Your life in property investment will not always run smoothly and there will be times when you have to put an incredible amount of time, energy, effort and money into a property only to realise the best course of action is to *walk away*. I know that sounds crazy, but it's true – it can happen. Every situation is different, of course, but the underlying truth remains the same: *you have to know when to quit*.

Knowing when to quit is damn hard. Sometimes you say to yourself, 'but . . . if I try it this way', 'if I try it that way', 'if I do this', 'if I do that . . .' Most likely you'll bend an ear or three of several friends and family members concerning your dilemma. But there will come a point when the options are limited and the rewards to be gained from a huge amount of effort and/or money and time are just not there. You have to balance your books. You have to balance what you're putting in against what you're getting out.

Such problems can happen even before a property acquisition – you really want the property, for example, but cannot run the numbers to make the deal stack. Unless you want to commit financial suicide, you have to walk away. Similarly, you may get involved in a price war over a property – the competition heats up and the property is no longer the deal it once was. Paying more for an asset just to win the battle will do you no favours – it will simply take you many more years to recoup your investment. Maybe in the long term the extra money paid will be worth it – but only you will know the price at which a property makes sense for you.

Sometimes you will need to walk away even when you own an asset. Maybe it no longer makes financial sense to keep it – it's underwater or it's losing you money. Or maybe your money just isn't working as hard for you as it could be. It could be a property you invested in a long time ago that has increased in value, but where the rental yields no longer make financial sense and the equity stake isn't being used to its fullest capability. You will have to ask yourself: do I need to walk away from this now? Could my money be put to better use elsewhere?

All the while you will be trying to balance your books, thinking about the funds you have and trying to make the most of them against your investment goals and the effort input these require of you. The key thing to bear in mind is: success is about choosing what to *stop* doing, as much as it is about choosing what to *start* doing.

Go For It!

Write a stop list. What can you STOP doing to free up more time, energy and funds?

PART FOUR: CUSTOMER RULES

Every investor needs customers if they are to succeed. Whether you are selling or renting property, you need somebody to give you money in exchange if you are to make a commercial success of your venture. Customer Rules looks at the 'people part' of the business, that is, the people who you will need to satisfy if you are to succeed. Everybody has their own style of how they deal with customers, but there are key principles that underpin successful property management. The saying goes: 'the customer is always right'; I would say the customer is *usually* right. But regardless of who is right, the buck, and the *bucks*, always stop with you.

So take the time to work on your Customer Rules and how you want to manage and deal with people, and let's get you started with being the Customer Champion you were born to be.

Rule 76: Know your role as a landlord

Your role as the landlord is to ensure you are providing the service your customers need.

How you manage your properties will very much depend on you, how you are as a person and how you want to run your business. Some landlords have no interest in running their properties and instruct agents from the day dot, while others want full hands-on day-to-day involvement and prefer to lay their own roof tiles than give any business to an outside agent. Then you have the landlords in between who like to mix it up and run some of the business themselves, while seeking outside help for other parts. There is no right or wrong way – the most important thing is to do what you feel comfortable doing.

Being a successful landlord requires you to identify, understand and meet the demands of the market. It is about choosing who you want to do business with and ensuring you have the right property with the right customers and the right service to meet their needs. Property investment relies on customers to make it a commercial success. Landlords need good, paying customers if they are to draw an income from the property. Any landlord who has ever had the misfortune of dealing with non-paying, difficult or even absconding tenants will understand how important good customers are.

Tenants can make or break a landlord, and their importance in the success of property investment should never be underestimated. This means, from the outset, tenants need to be looked after as customers. If they are to remain long term and loyal, it is critical their needs are served and that any repairs or issues are resolved satisfactorily and promptly. It is sometimes said that workers leave bosses rather than jobs, and much the same can be said in relation to property: tenants leave landlords rather than properties. While tenants can sometimes be overly demanding, it is important to always have an open dialogue. A tenant who feels they are not being listened to, or whose needs are not being met, will soon start to look elsewhere to find satisfaction.

Your role as the landlord is to ensure you are providing the product and service your customers need. If you do not have the time or wherewithal to do this, it is advisable to instruct a professional who can. Being a landlord is a customer-focused service. You may have invested in property; however, that is just half the story – the other half to making property investment a success lies in the management and maintenance of your asset.

Go For It!

Evaluate how much time and energy you have for managing a property investment. Can you really provide the service your customers need?

Rule 77: Get to know your customers

Who do you want to rent to?

The tenant market comprises a range of different people with various needs and wants. Few investors are big enough to supply the needs of an entire market, so it makes sense to segment the market into different customer groups and identify those you can best serve – or who you would most like to do business with.

It is important to remember that people choose properties based on a perceived fit with themselves. This means you should think carefully about the types of people your property will attract, or indeed what sorts of people you *want* your property to attract. If you want to appeal successfully to a particular market segments it is critical you have the right property to appeal to the right people. This means you need to ask yourself: *who do I want to rent to?*

In thinking about who you want to rent to, you will need to get to know your customers. One simple way of doing this is to put together a customer profile. Many big businesses use customer profiles to help them target their products and services more effectively, and there is no reason why you cannot take a tip from the big boys. The sorts of things your customer profile should include are:

- Age, sex, relationship status.
- Employment status and earnings (both current and future).

- Life trajectory so far (e.g. attended university, relationship breakdown, etc.).

- Property trajectory so far (e.g. previous homeowner, first-time renter).

- Property aspirations (e.g. wants to buy own property).

- Financial status (e.g. ability to own home, savings).

- Life desires (e.g. plans for the future, including marriage, kids or career ambitions).

- Leisure pursuits (e.g. enjoys working out at gym, eating out, socialising).

- Family and friends (e.g. desire to be close to kin).

- Amenity requirements (e.g. close to school, shops).

- Area wanted (e.g. close to park, low crime rate).

- Transport connections (e.g. road and rail links).

- Property needs (e.g. home office, off-street car parking).

- Property requirements (e.g. power shower, modern fixtures and fittings).

By putting together a consumer profile, you will be able to 'get under the skin' of your target market and gain an insight into their property requirements. This will enable you to select the type of property that will appeal to the type of tenant you wish to attract.

Go For It!

Start drawing up a consumer profile of your ideal tenant. If you have magazines and papers to hand, cut out images and create a collage of what your ideal tenant's life is like.

Rule 78: Find your niche

Having targeted market knowledge means you can focus and maximise resources, which, in turn, leads to better property investments.

'*Who* do I want to do business with?'

This question often gets overlooked in favour of: '*What* property do I want to buy?' or 'What property can I *afford* to buy?' However, what you need to remember is that the type of property you choose will ultimately dictate the type of people you will be dealing with. Customer types vary, and I can tell you from experience that it's very difficult to be 'all things to all people'. Trying to please everybody is a strain on resources; a more effective use of time and money is to identify and target a type of customer, such as families or students, and get to know them and their needs – better than they know them themselves!

The most successful investors I know are those who focused on one or two market segments. They specialised in building a focused portfolio and a body of knowledge that led to enhanced market understanding, improved properties and specific management systems. If you speak to many long-term and medium-size investors, you will find that most have identified a segment that works for them and that they stick to. Having targeted market knowledge means you can focus and maximise resources, which, in turn, leads to better property investments.

To find your niche, you need to think about your goals and find a strategy that fits with who you are and how you want to make your investment work. Not everybody wants to be hands-on and not everybody wants to build an empire. Knowing your core strategy, the types of people you want to do business with and what factors are important to you, means you can define which properties are of interest. Once you know what you are looking for, you can set your search criteria, give agents clear briefs and set up automatic alerts. A clear and focused search means you can make quicker and better-informed decisions that will enable you to grow your business more effectively.

Over time, you will become more skilled in dealing with your market sector and will understand the product and service levels you need to provide. This creates confidence and expertise, and means you can compete on a higher level because you know what your market needs and wants and can cater specifically for it. Investing in this way is not only more effective, it is also more satisfactory and enjoyable. And, while, over time, your strategy may change and evolve, the most important thing is to have a strategy to start with!

Go For It!

Ask yourself: 'Who do you want to do business with?' Think about this question and consider your objectives and your likes and dislikes. Write down your answer.

Rule 79: Have a Property Manual

A 'Property Manual' provides key information to tenants on how to live in the property and what to do when things go wrong.

Imagine buying a new computer or any other appliance and not having an operating manual. What would you do if you had a problem? You would turn to the manual! Manuals provide information, troubleshooting tips and advice on how to operate a product. This is what a 'Property Manual' does – it provides key information to tenants on how to live in the property and what to do when things go wrong. The Property Manual is your best friend – it is your 'User's Guide' to the property.

The Property Manual does not have to be fancy – an A4 binder with plastic sleeve pockets is more than enough. The most important thing is the information it contains – and the more you provide, the less questions and issues will arise.

A Property Manual will typically include:

- Instructions on what to do in an emergency (e.g. if you smell gas who to call, contractor emergency contact details).

- The location of the stopcock and how to turn it.

- The location of the fuse box and an explanation of the main fuses and what to do if they trip, plus instructions on how to change them.

- The location of the mains gas and how to turn it off.

- The location of electric, gas and water meters and, where possible, supplier details.

- The location of smoke detectors and a reminder to check the batteries are working.

- The contact telephone numbers for service providers (e.g. council, waste collection).

- Local information about council tax bands, refuse collection days and local doctors.

- Photocopies of instruction manuals for the boiler and any appliances (e.g. washing machine, cooker, dishwasher). If you do not have these, they are usually available to download from the internet by inputting the make and model number.

- Photocopies of any warranties for products in the property, or service agreements (e.g. alarm, boiler).

- Copies of the Gas Safe certificate, EPC and electrical certificate.

- A simple overview of how things work (e.g. window locks, alarm).

- Maintenance tips (e.g. how to prevent mould, how to clean washing machine filters).

- Troubleshooting tips for when something does not work as expected (e.g. how to relight the boiler).

- How to live in and be aware of the property and what to report (e.g. leaking overflow, flaking paint, damp patches, blocked guttering).

- Information for when the tenant is leaving the property unoccupied, such as going on holiday.

- Information for when you (as the landlord) are on holiday and who to contact in your absence.

Having a Property Manual will equip customers with the information required concerning how to live in the property, and will ensure they are prepared for when issues arise and know how to deal with them promptly and effectively.

Go For It!

Put together a Property Manual for your property with the information detailed above.

Rule 80: Get organised

*To ensure the smooth running of
a property, you need to run it like
a business.*

Owning property produces paperwork like nobody's business, and if you want to get on in this game you are going to have to get organised and quickly. While property investment is a fun business to be in, it's also serious – and it comes with a shedload of responsibility. Knowing what bills you need to pay and when, what monies are due in and when, what insurance to pay, what regulations to abide by, what records to keep and for how long are some of the most tedious yet important parts of the job.

To get organised, you have to be on top of your calendar. A calendar is a crucial tool for both recurring dates such as rent and mortgage payments and for scheduling dates such as mortgage product expirations, Gas Safe checks, AST expiry dates and appointments to meet contractors. As in the Rule 'Cash flow is king' (Rule 54), you need to know what your cash flow position is at any given time of the month. This means knowing when payments are due in and when they are due out. These should always be scheduled and checked to ensure they are correct. There are many accounting software packages on the market; however, a simple Excel spreadsheet can suffice as long as it is tallied with a calendar.

All data, including your calendar and banking, should be available online so that you always have instant access to your schedule from anywhere in the world.

To ensure the smooth running of a property, you need to run it like a business. Every property should be treated like a mini-business of its own. This means that each property needs a separate file, including paperwork such as the purchase and finance documents, contract documentation such as the AST, EPCs, inventory, Gas Safe, tenant and agent details, and any other property-related information. A copy of the Property Manual should also be kept on file along with a list of preferred contractors. It's best to set up a separate bank account for your property investments rather than using your personal account, and this should mean your accounts are quicker and easier to maintain.

Getting organised also means monitoring your investments and ensuring they are performing as expected. Market research of comparable properties should be undertaken every quarter and the notes kept on file. Any major deviations should be analysed and your position reviewed to assess if action is required (e.g. increase rent, sell property). The system you choose does not have to be complicated or take a long time – the most important things are that you keep it up to date and keep all your paperwork together!

Go For It!

Create a property file. Collate all information for a property. Mark on a calendar all important dates such as rent due, AST expiration, insurance renewal, etc.

Rule 81: Check out your customers

Never feel desperate or pressurised
to rent to someone you instinctively
feel uncomfortable with, or who
does not bode well.

Unfortunately, most businesses at some point will experience a bad customer, and property investment is not immune to this. However, there are ways to try to reduce the possibilities of this happening, and in my experience the best prevention is through comprehensive tenant referencing. This can be undertaken yourself or by using a professional referencing agency. The first part of the screening is to check a tenant's rental history through current and previous landlord references. If you are in any doubt, or have difficulty obtaining a reference, it is possible to request to visit a tenant's current rental property to check the standards. I have done this myself on a couple of occasions when I was unsure of a tenant, and this home visit enabled me to assess the situation better.

Checking that a tenant can afford to rent your property is vital. This means looking at their latest three months' bank statements and actually checking and analysing how they run their account. Look to see if there are any returned payments. Are they overdrawn? Identify the rent payments going out every month and ensure they are regular. Check that any monies they claim to be receiving are being credited to their account. Get their latest three pay slips or housing benefit payments and check these against their bank statements. Is the money they claim they are receiving being paid into the same bank account? If not, ask questions why. Never be afraid to talk about money – unless they demonstrably have the income needed to pay the rent on your property, you should not take the risk of allowing them to move in.

Get a full financial picture of their situation. Understand what credit cards or loans they have. Carry out a credit check and ensure they have a good history. If not, ask them why – question them about any financial issues they have had in the past and how they were resolved. Check with their employers if any changes may be made to their working arrangements in the next twelve months. Understand who in their network may help them financially if they run into trouble. If in doubt, seek a guarantor who will guarantee the rent if the tenant defaults. Make sure you take a deposit to cover at least one month's rent – preferably two. Ask questions, request proof and analyse their set-up. Never feel desperate or pressurised to rent to someone you instinctively feel uncomfortable with, or who does not bode well. A vacancy is always preferable over a bad tenant, as an empty property is unlikely to cost you as much as the latter. If in any doubt about an applicant, do not proceed. Choose your customers wisely and protect your business interests through thorough and prudent screening.

Go For It!

Call three letting agencies and ask them about their tenant referencing procedures. What are they doing to ensure the quality of their tenants?

Rule 82: Choose a great agent

How your agent presents themselves and your property are a key part of securing a successful sale or let.

Great agents are worth their weight in gold. Even if you are intending to sell or rent a property yourself, you will usually still need an agent to get you listed on the top websites. Getting the right maximum exposure is critical and the agent you choose is a vital part of your future success. I am always amazed at the number of people who choose agents just on the basis of price alone, rather than looking at the service levels they and their potential customers will receive. How your agent presents themselves and your property are a key part of securing a successful sale or let.

Estate agents can make or break a property sale. It doesn't matter how fabulous your property is; if the agent never answers any enquiries, you don't have much hope of making a sale. The same goes for not chasing feedback from viewings to not even progressing a sale. Many a sale gets lost in the process due to lazy and inept agents and it is important to ensure your property is not one of them. Choosing an estate agent based on excellent customer service and recent successful sales in the local area is critical. 'Sold' boards are a great indicator of how well an estate agent is performing. However, what is even better is getting the opinion of current vendors who are selling/have sold with the agents in question. It will require a dash of courage, but knocking on the door of a 'Sold' property and talking with people about their experiences is a great way for you to gain insight. If this approach seems rather too cavalier, you can find review sites for agents online, which can be a gold-mine of information.

When employing the services of a letting agent, it is critical to verify the service levels on offer. Given that the agent will be responsible for handling the financial side of the property along with the ongoing maintenance, it is essential they have the skills required. Property management is a very labour-intensive and stressful profession and requires a broad skill-set to deal with the issues. Property managers not only need to be diplomatic and assertive when dealing with tenants, they also need to be exceptionally charming and very pragmatic. Plus, you have to trust your letting agent to look after an incredibly expensive asset. All this should not be taken lightly, and rigorous and thorough research should be undertaken before parting with your keys.

While price plays an important role in selecting which agent to employ, the service you and your customers receive is the most important aspect. It is the end customers who will be paying for your product, so how agents treat customers should be tested via a 'mystery shop'. This experience will quickly tell you whether or not you have found a great agent!

Go For It!

Find a property for sale or rent and call the agent as if you are an interested person. Time how long it takes for them to answer the phone and connect you to the right person. Ask lots of questions about the property and test how they respond. How much knowledge does the agent have? How interested do they sound? How helpful are they? Do they make you want to view the property? Rate your experience and then call another agent in the local area. Do this for three agents and compare your notes. Which agent made you feel they wanted your business?

Rule 83: Be the Amazon of customer service

Offering exceptional customer service means being trusted and relied upon to deliver solutions.

Amazon are renowned for their exceptional customer service. Problems are sorted quickly and effectively with minimal hassle. In fact, their problem-solving ability makes you feel like you never had a problem in the first place. Their service is trusted and reliable. When you purchase a product from Amazon, you know you are going to get great service. Even if along the way, or later down the line, you have problems, Amazon have the resources to sort it. And that level of service makes you feel good; you feel prepared to pay that little bit extra and it makes you confident that you can rely on them to sort out any issues you may encounter.

Being the Amazon of the rental market is not an easy feat. However, exceptional customer service pays dividends. Not only does a high level of customer service mean you retain more customers and enhance loyalty – it also makes for less problems in the end. Tenants who have faith in their landlords to sort problems quickly and effectively actually cause fewer problems. Problems do not escalate. Problems get fixed. The problems that did arise are quickly forgotten – they were fixed so quickly and effortlessly that they didn't even appear on the customer radar. And, even if they do, they are remembered for the service that was provided: the solution.

Offering exceptional customer service means being trusted and relied upon to deliver solutions. As the Amazon of customer service, you cannot prevent problems from happening – problems happen and that is a fact of life. But the difference is that you're *prepared* for the problems, ready to provide the solutions and fix them. This line of thinking requires a change in mentality. It requires an acceptance and appreciation of your role as the troubleshooter. To provide exceptional customer service means you must always be ready to deliver the solutions to the best of your ability.

Providing exceptional customer service can be time-consuming. This is why you should take a leaf out of Amazon's book: encourage customers to email you as the first point of call. This may sound simple, but using email as a preferred method of contact for routine maintenance requests and administrative queries is incredibly time effective and far more productive than fielding telephone calls. Emails can be looked at and actioned every hour of the day, they create an instant date-stamped record of events that can be retrieved and checked again at any time, and the contents can be quickly and easily copied to create task lists and jobs for contractors. Telephone calls tend to take longer and do not always focus on the issue at hand. Following the call, notes will need to be taken from the call – tasks created, details captured and actions implemented. The other drawback is that calls can only be made during set hours of the day – and it's not always convenient to talk. Emails are best used as the first point of contact, with telephones used sparingly, and mainly as the emergency contact.

To be the Amazon of customer service – you need to start from the right place: change your mentality and be ready to provide solutions.

Go For It!

Set up an email address for your tenants to contact you on. Write them a letter that states that all routine maintenance requests and administrative queries will be dealt with by email. Inform them that the telephone is for emergency use only.

Rule 84: Know when to listen and when to act

Listening to problems first and interrogating them, rather than jumping to act, is a skill that every property investor needs to develop early on.

When a customer has a problem it's very easy to rush off and start doing things. It doesn't matter what, but if you're *doing* something then you're obviously helping to fix the problem, right? Wrong. Not every problem needs a repairman or a contractor to attend. Not every problem is the landlord's responsibility. And not every problem can be answered in one or has an immediate solution. Indeed, not every problem is about the property: it could be health issues, job worries, schooling problems, or maybe even a disagreement with the neighbours. Problems are not always as easy to identify as you may think.

So how can you know when a problem *is* a problem? You have to listen carefully, ask questions and use your powers of analysis. I have often found that the problem that was originally reported was not in fact *the* problem. However, the only way I was able to understand what was the actual problem was by asking more questions. For example, a tenant contacted me recently to report a damp patch on the bedroom wall. He wanted me to send a damp specialist to fix the problem and then a decorator to paint over it. I thought carefully and asked several more questions. This culminated in my identifying the real problem, which was the blocked guttering outside the bedroom wall. A damp specialist was not required – but somebody to clear the gutter was!

Listening to problems first and interrogating them, rather than jumping to act, is a skill that every property investor needs to develop early on. The customer is not always right – and you will need to troubleshoot your way through and take the initiative to get to the root of the problem. Even if you are not technical – common-sense questions should be applied and issues probed deeper. It is only through identifying and gaining an understanding of what the real problem is that you can then act appropriately. Acting without fully knowing what the issue is can land you with a bunch of very expensive repair bills!

Go For It!

Next time somebody tells you a problem they have (and this doesn't have to be property related at all), notice how you react. Listen to yourself as you ask more questions, and delve deeper to try to understand what the actual problem is.

Rule 85: You don't have to be best mates

Friendly is fine, friends is not.

Your tenants are your customers. They are not your friends, nor should you aim to make them your friends. That is not to say you can't be friendly (you really *should* be friendly) but there is a major difference between being friendly and being friends. Friendly is fine, friends is not.

Keeping a fair distance to allow personal and professional relations to develop is key to long-lasting tenant–investor relations. Just because you're the landlord doesn't give you any automatic right to respect. You may be the landlord and in a position of authority, but respect must be earned. Respect is earned from treating customers fairly and appropriately. It is also earned by sorting out problems promptly and efficiently.

Respect is lost when you don't respect your customers. Listening to your customers is critical. Even if you don't agree with what they're saying, you should communicate the reasons for your disagreement politely and justly. Though some will tell you, 'the customer is always right', there is another saying: 'give them an inch and they will take a mile'. Be wary when tenants try to overstep the mark and be clear about your position.

Building open and honest communication with customers enables you to create a strong working partnership – and it *is* a partnership. Your tenants have made a home in your property and they pay you rent every month for the privilege – and you need that rent. Property investment – especially when you're renting property – is a two-way street: you need your tenants as much as they need you (and your property). That is why this situation demands mutual respect.

Relationships need work, and, like the property itself, will require maintenance. It doesn't take much to remember to send a Christmas card, or to ask occasionally how your tenants are as people, not just as customers. It can feel hard sometimes when you have your own stuff going on, but don't forget your customers are also real people with real lives outside of living in your property. Take an interest in them, ask about how they are, how work is going, how little Jimmy is getting on (it's always good if you remember the names of any kids or pets, so write them down, together with other key points about your tenants, and keep them on file to nudge your memory). It doesn't have to be a conversation in great detail or to take a lot of time, but it's important to show you care – and for you to know you care. Your customers are part and parcel of your property investment, so make sure you are personable and professional in all your dealings.

Go For It!

If you have a tenant in occupation, give them a ring now and ask them how they are. Write down any details of names and events they refer to and add these to the property file.

Rule 86: Get a (private) life!

Boundaries demarcate what is your personal life and what is your professional life.

In the desire to be the best property investor in town, boundaries can easily be forgotten. But, even if this is your full-time job, it is important to have boundaries. Boundaries demarcate what is your *personal* life and what is your *professional* life. And no matter how much you love property investment and how much you want to make it a part of your personal life, I would advise you to maintain your investments as a professional interest. Your properties are your business, they are what you do, they are a part of you – but that does not *make* them you.

Creating and maintaining a separation between you and your properties is actually much harder than most people realise. In the desire to be a great investor and have high levels of customer service, you can quickly find yourself running around trying to please everyone. In the beginning, being at a tenant's beck and call may seem like a novelty and a dream you wish to fulfil – it may even make you feel valued and important. However, property has a habit of taking over your life and, unless you protect your *personal* time, any privacy or space you thought you once had can quickly evaporate.

Rules and boundaries need to be put in place from the

outset, and, if you haven't done this yet, I would advise you to do so as quickly as possible. Boundaries should be clearly stated up front and separate telephone numbers and email addresses should be used for your property management and personal life. Maintaining a professional and office-like approach means you make tenants aware of your usual business hours and your preferred method of contact. An out-of-office-hours number should be provided for emergency use only, with the proviso that any misuse or abuse of the number could result in a penalty fine being applied. To succeed in property investment, you need to run it and treat it as a business, however much you like what you do. Separation of your personal life from your professional life is key to long-term business success.

Go For It!

If you haven't already, buy a different telephone number and register a different email address solely for your tenants' use. Work out your office hours and inform tenants of these. Provide them with an out-of-hours contact number for emergency use only.

Rule 87: Have some respect!

Respect is a state of mind and
a way of being.

It still surprises me the number of landlords I come across who have the wrong attitude to being a landlord. And when I say the wrong attitude, I mean the *wrong* attitude. They are the landlords who give the rest of us in the business a bad name. They are the sort of landlords who, because they own property, think they have a right to enter at any time of the day and night, despite people living there; the sort you see on the news who couldn't be bothered to fix broken heating systems, who allowed their tenants to freeze, who ignored basic safety warnings and who, in a word, should not be in the business.

Thankfully, they are in the minority, and most landlords are in the business to be a *good* landlord. Good landlords understand the rules of the game. They understand that property investment is a long-term business and know that their tenants are their customers, so they treat them with respect. They respect the tenant's right to privacy – to live in a safe, secure and habitable home – and they recognise that these rights are enshrined in law, each covered in the Assured Shorthold Contract (AST) signed with the tenant. However, having a contract is one thing, respecting the terms and adhering to them is another.

Respect isn't just about what is written and agreed in a contract. There is also respect for your customers *as* your customers. There is respect for having them in your life and in your property; for them paying the rent every month and on time; for them looking after the property; for them telling you when something is not working and being available for a contractor to attend; for them making your property their home. But I think you get the gist – respect is *much* bigger than what is contained in the rental agreement. Respect is a state of mind and a way of being.

Treating your customers, your property and your business with respect instils respect. People will see that you hold yourself, and them, in high regard and they will look to give you respect back. Creating a respectful relationship starts on day one of your tenancy and, at the outset, the Rules of respecting the property and their relationship with you needs to be explained. Standards, expectations and service levels should be openly discussed. This is the start of the Rules of respect – and from here on in, that relationship needs to be nurtured and fed. Respect is a movable feast – and you need to be sure you are *earning*, not losing, that of your customer.

Go For It!

Think about someone you respect. Write down the reasons why they inspire respect in you. What can you learn from them and apply to you?

Rule 88: Keep your door open

Being a landlord means you are not only a product owner but also a service provider.

Everyone has their ups and downs. Life can be tough going at times and plain sailing at others. In the easy times when everything is going great, we don't need or want for much, but in the more difficult moments it's sometimes hard to know who to call on when things go wrong. Who can you talk to when you've lost your job, split from your partner, or you're not sure how to make ends meet? This stuff of life happens often and, as the landlord, it is likely to be you who can help a tenant more than anybody else in such situations.

Being a landlord means you are not only a product owner but also a service provider – and the service you provide to your customers is critical if you want them to remain with you long term. Operating an 'open-door' policy does not mean your customers have *carte blanche* to call you about every little thing that happens in their life. However, keeping an open door means you are available to listen to their problems should they potentially affect you or the property. This will mean you are more likely to be on their list of people to call when things do go wrong.

So why would you want to be on that list? Frankly, it's

an early warning sign and will give you the heads-up to any issues that may arise due to the situation. For example, when one of my tenants was made redundant from her City job, I was the second person she called after her mum. This early information gave me the opportunity to plan next steps and understand how to manage the tenancy for the best going forwards.

As a landlord, your role and job remit is pretty broad, and sometimes being a social worker and life coach is called for – along with being a complete pragmatist and a very good paper-shuffler! Tenants who know they can talk to you and be honest and upfront are far more likely to involve you early on. They will look to you for assistance, and, although you may not be able to help every time, it is critical to show a willingness to help.

Helping tenants through difficult times is imperative to successful property management. It is important to remember that the landlord–tenant relationship is a *partnership* and one that needs to be worked on together. If a tenant loses their job, or a relationship breaks down, it is in your best interests to assist them as much as possible. Operating an open-door policy is more likely to encourage your tenants to talk to you, and the more they talk to you, the more you can help them – and help your business.

Go For It!

Arrange an inspection at your property and talk to your tenants. Make sure they know that your door is always open, and encourage them to call you if they ever find themselves in difficult situations, confident that you will try your best to help.

Rule 89: Don't be a doormat

Not everyone is going to like you
and what you do.

Pretty much everyone wants to be liked. It's far easier to go through life being liked and liking people than the other way round. Not liking people takes up a lot of energy and negative emotions and doesn't really get you anywhere – apart from not being liked. But there are times when you are going to have to *do* something, or *be* someone, that will *not* be liked. It's hard and can be uncomfortable, but life is tough and you are going to have to get over it – not everyone is going to like you and what you do.

So how do you get used to not being liked? I don't know if you ever really get used to it, but I think you become more accepting. You understand that you have to separate an action from a person – I may do something you do not like, but that does not mean I am a dislikeable person. For example, I may have to ask a tenant for rent that is overdue when they have a million other bills to pay. The tenant may not like me asking for the overdue rent, and I may not like asking – but that does not make me a dislikeable person. You see, there is a difference between what someone *does* and what someone *is*. This distinction is very important to remember: *the action is different from the person.*

The reason this is important is that there will come a time when you will have to say or do things to your customers that they will not like. They will tell you they don't like them, and they may even say they don't like you. That can be hard, especially when you are trying to be the Amazon of customer service. However, there is a difference between exceptional customer service and being a doormat. At times, this difference may seem very small; however, it is an important distinction nonetheless and one you should be aware of.

Saying 'no' is much harder than saying 'yes'. Saying 'no' often involves having to explain the reasons for your answer. A request from a tenant along the lines of, 'My kitchen is really old, can you get me a new one?' may seem reasonable enough. If you have the money saved in the bank and the expense is worth the effort, you may well say 'yes'. But what do you do if you don't have the money, if you think the tenant is being unreasonable, or if the works are not worth the outlay? Your answer will probably be 'no'. And you will then have to explain why your answer is 'no'. Your tenant will probably not like your answer and you will need to be prepared for that – they may even leave on account of it. But not installing a new kitchen when a tenant requests one does not make you a bad person (unless you do not have a functioning, serviceable kitchen – in which case you should jolly well do it straightaway!). It just means you do not have the resources, or the job is not as much a priority for you as it is for the tenant.

Understanding it's OK to *not* be liked, or to make decisions that will *not* be liked, is part and parcel of being a property investor. Saying 'no' is just as important a part of the business as saying 'yes'. The key to success lies in knowing which to say and when.

Go For It!

Practise saying 'no'. Next time you are asked to do something that you do not want to do, just say 'no' and explain your reasons why.

Rule 90: No pay . . . no stay

A tenant not paying their rent is the equivalent of your boss not paying your salary.

For the most part, customers understand this essential Rule: rent gets paid in return for living in your property. However, at times this Rule can be forgotten, misunderstood or just plain ignored. Customers not adhering to this Rule can be a major source of frustration, anxiety and several sleepless nights. Many investors have lending on their property, with mortgages and loans to pay every month – a large chunk of which gets paid from customers' rents. Non-paying customers are therefore a major issue to investors and need to be dealt with quickly and effectively.

Chasing customer debt is one of the least welcome parts of the job – and it can be one of the most stressful. Customers will come up with a barrage of reasons and excuses as to why rent has not been paid. However, a tenant not paying their rent is the equivalent of your boss not paying your salary. Now, when you look at it like that, how often would you be willing to go to work and not be paid your salary as agreed? Not often, I would have thought! This is how you need to approach the subject of non-paying customers: a *tenant not paying their rent is like your boss not paying your salary*. Now you understand the importance of this

Rule – and it is an essential *Rule* – it is time to get tough and take action.

Procedures need to be in place so that you know instantly the moment a customer falls behind with their rent. These don't have to be anything fancy – a simple note on the calendar every month will suffice. The key lies in checking the rent has been received and, if not, taking appropriate steps to rectify the situation immediately. Allowing rent to go unpaid for long periods of time not only sends the signal you don't really need the money, but it also makes it incredibly difficult for customers to catch up and get back into credit. Debt can quickly spiral out of control – remember, if your rent has gone unpaid, it's likely other bills the tenant is liable for may also have not been paid. This could potentially mean you are joining a queue of debtors, and you need to make sure you are at the head of the queue!

Everyone needs a roof over their head, but tenants can sometimes forget just how vital it is to have somewhere to live. When rent goes unpaid, you may need to remind them of that, making it clear that they must keep up with their payments if they wish to continue living in your property. This may sound overly harsh; however, unless you want to start your own housing charity, you'd be best advised to keep on top of debtors. People not paying the rent means you will be footing the bill, and unless you can manage non-payers yourself you will probably end up paying a solicitor to sort it out at court.

Go For It!

Check the calendar and mark when rent is due. Set a reminder to check the bank that day. If the rent is not received, contact the tenant immediately to clarify the situation.

Rule 91: Avoid too many 'sun-downers'

Avoiding the voids should be your number-one priority when looking to rent out a property.

Voids are an investor's worst enemy. Lost rent is lost revenue that can never be got back, no matter how hard you try. Vacancies cost money. Even when a property has no finance loaned against it, voids lose you money, not only through failing to make you money, but through incurring costs and bills that you will be liable for while the property is sitting idle. Remember: *empty properties are expensive properties.* Think of it as a 'sun-downer': every time the sun goes down on your empty property, your money expires and it can never be recouped.

Avoiding the voids should be your number-one priority when looking to rent out a property. Finding suitable tenants should be treated as an urgent matter, so, once a notice to leave has been received, marketing should begin in earnest. Enquiries and viewings should be actively monitored and, where appropriate, the price amended to ensure you have a good selection of quality tenants. On some occasions, it may be necessary to lower the rent; it is often cheaper in the long run to take a reduced rent than to have a longer vacancy.

Moreover, rents can always be reviewed later in the tenancy.

In addition to lost revenue, the cost of having an empty property quickly mounts up. Insurance premiums usually rise to cover the increased risk of an empty property, while the cover offered will tend to lower. Council tax and utility bills will also become your liability when you do not have a tenant in occupation. On top of this, there are the things about a property that may go unnoticed when people do not live there – a small leak in a pipe can quickly cause untold damage to a property when it is not fixed. You also have security issues when a property is vacant; with nobody living there, it becomes a more obvious target for miscreants.

The simple fact is that properties need to be lived in. Vacant properties soon fall into disrepair. The law of entropy, albeit simplified, means that, if you are not putting energy into something to keep it in order, it's going to get worse. Properties, even when left unoccupied, do not remain the same. Paint peels, wood rots, metal rusts, gardens overgrow, and properties that were once wonderful homes soon look shabby. Avoiding the voids is critical to long-term invest-ment success, and remember: every sundown is lost revenue that you will never be able to recoup.

Go For It!

Use a calculator to work out the cost of a void in comparison to taking a reduced rent.

Rule 92: Reward loyalty

Once you have a good customer, you should do all you can to keep them.

It's popularly quoted in business that it costs five times more to acquire a new customer than to retain an existing one, and I can well believe this cost principle would apply to property investment. Once you take into account the agency fees, voids and property upgrade costs, not to mention the hassle and risks involved in taking on new tenants, it's likely to be much cheaper to keep your existing good ones. Good, loyal and long-term customers are critical to building a successful property business. You should make it your mission to attract and retain the best customers to your property.

Good customers are worth their weight in gold; they pay your rent on time and they look after your property. Once you have a good customer, you should do all you can to keep them. One way to ensure you do so is to abide by the Rule 'Be the Amazon of customer service' (Rule 83); another way is by *rewarding* them. Rewards speak volumes and show your tenants how much you value them. Feeling valued helps keep customers loyal and reduces the risk of their seeking out alternatives – your competition.

How do you reward loyalty? The most valuable reward for most customers is via their pocket. That means real money and real cost savings. Keeping your rent purposely just below the going market rate and informing tenants you are doing so, *because they are such good tenants*, makes them feel valued and keeps more money in their pocket. Price rises are invariably unwelcome, so softening the blow with a below-market increase that reflects how much you want to keep their custom is more likely to retain tenants.

It can be very tempting to increase the rent (especially if prices have risen); but don't forget that once an increase has been notified, your tenants will usually start to scout the local market to see what else is available. Unless they are particularly settled in your property or you are offering something difficult to beat, your price increase may potentially drive your customers into the arms of your competitors. Tenants do not often think about the additional costs associated with moving, let alone the hassle factor. The key thing that many of them see when a rent increase is proposed is the extra money they will have to find every month. That being the case, you should take time to consider how much a new customer is worth to you versus the cost of acquiring them, and stack that figure against the cost of retaining the customers you have. It is worth assessing if a retention strategy is more cost and time effective than an acquisition strategy, and you should plan your customer management accordingly.

Go For It!

Research the different loyalty schemes that companies use to retain customers. List the key features and see if you could use any of them in your business.

Rule 93: Know if and when to ask for more

It is important to remember that your tenants are your customers and, ideally, you would like them to remain so.

Keeping up to date with rental values is critical to knowing how your property is performing and whether more income could be extracted from your asset. A boom in the rental market means prices can change quite significantly in a short period of time; this is especially the case in some parts of London. It is advisable therefore to check the rental you are receiving against the current market rate. If there is a major discrepancy (up or down), you should investigate this further and find out the reasons for this. Rents can go down as well as up and it is important you are prepared for this should the tenant vacate.

If a rental property is let for noticeably less than the current market rate, the amount should be reviewed. If a tenant has vacated a property and there is going to be a new let, then the decision to increase the rent is a simple one: the rent should be increased in line with current market rates. However, if the property is currently tenanted, you should take into consideration a number of factors before increasing the rent.

- Check the Assured Shorthold Tenancy (AST) agreement to ensure you are permitted to increase the rent.

- Review your current tenants and assess their status. Consider such things as: the condition of the property and how they look after it, how long they have lived there, payment history, and how much you like doing business with them.

- Assess how your current tenants may react to a price increase. Can they afford for you to increase the rent? If the price increase may mean they can no longer afford the property, are you prepared to lose them as tenants?

- Calculate the cost of a new tenant. In addition to any letting fees and void periods, a property rented to a new tenant will most likely require additional works. Existing tenants can be quite forgiving of internal décor items; however, this is often not the case for new tenants, especially when you are looking to achieve a higher market rate.

- Evaluate if the hassle is worth the extra money? Consideration should be given to the time and costs involved in starting new tenancies. There are usually some issues that arise and these should be weighed up against existing tenancies, particularly if the current tenants have been in situ for a long period of time, are reliable and look after the property.

If, having assessed the market and reviewed your tenants, you feel a price increase is warranted, it is best to discuss this with them. In my experience, tenants want to feel part of the negotiation process rather than just being told of the new increased rent. It is important to remember that your tenants are your customers and, ideally, you would like them to remain so.

Personally, I am a strong believer in renting properties just below current market rates. This discounted pricing strategy ensures my rents are competitive and, I have found, tends to attract longer-term tenants. Moreover, the cost savings enjoyed by the tenants mean they are more likely to spend additional funds on enhancing a property. This strategy has rewarded me well with the majority of my tenants staying with me for many years.

Go For It!

Calculate how much it would cost to attract a new tenant on a higher rent versus retaining a current customer on a lower rent. Ensure you factor in all expenses, including void periods, agency fees, utility bills and any improvement work that may be necessary.

Rule 94: Create scarcity

Scarcity works by motivating people to act quicker; this can lead to increased levels of demand and perceptions of value.

Scarcity is a well-known marketing strategy for increasing demand and perceived value. When a product or service is scarce, or perceived as scarce, and there is a limited time to act, people feel motivated by a sense of urgency and tend to act quicker for fear of losing out. This threat of a 'potential loss' makes the restricted item even more important to people. Potentially losing something before they've even had an opportunity to possess it drives people to action. This tendency is known as 'reactance'. Reactance occurs when you feel someone or something is taking away your choices or limiting the range of alternatives. The Rule of Scarcity works because people feel that they will lose their opportunity to act unless they do so immediately. This means they are driven to acquire something to alleviate the threat of potential loss.

Exploiting people's response to scarcity is a well-known tactic and one often employed by blue-chip household companies, but how can you use this strategy in property investment?

There are various ways you can create scarcity, or the perception of scarcity:

- Provide a property that has something unique that your target audience values, and will find hard to resist and difficult to locate elsewhere (e.g. a top-of-the-range kitchen with high-specification appliances).

- Position the property to ensure your target market understands how scarce the offer is, by using wording such as 'rarely on the market', 'first time on the market'.

- Set a higher-than-usual price for the property to capture a premium price-point. Usually, a scarce supply and high demand will mean customers are willing to pay a higher price for the product.

- Alternatively, set a discounted price to increase the odds of a quick sale or let and to encourage a 'must-see-it-now' mentality.

- Promote the need for people to act quickly by using words in your advertising such as 'first to see will buy'.

- Restrict and/or limit people's choices in the availability of viewing times. People want what they can't have and, if they are told a property may soon be unavailable, the desire to view will increase, as will the urgency to act.

- Create allure by increasing the perception of competition. Conduct block viewings at set times to heighten interest. People who feel they are competing for a limited resource will be more motivated to take action.

- Create deadlines by which people need to act; for example, offers must be submitted within twenty-four hours for consideration.

- Point out the potential loss of *not* acting. People overvalue what you are restricting – the fear of loss is an overwhelming feeling that motivates people to act.

Scarcity works by motivating people to act quicker; this can lead to increased levels of demand and perceptions of value. Of course, not all customers appreciate and value scarcity, and this tactic may turn off some clients. However, when executed well, scarcity builds a sense of urgency that motivates people to act quicker and value your property higher.

Go For It!

Look at some of the advertising promotions used by companies trying to create a sense of scarcity. Learn from the language, tactics and positioning they use and see how you can employ these in your business.

Rule 95: Offer something extra

Every business needs to attract the
right kind of customers and
get them to sign up.

Everybody loves a free gift. Free gifts are well known in the marketing world for attracting customers. Don't worry at this moment. I am not suggesting you offer your property for free! But you can learn from the world of marketing and offer your property in such a way that customers feel they are getting something *extra* with you. And that something extra could be just the difference between why they take *your* property over the competition.

The property market is a fast-moving arena and properties that are hanging around need to be looked at carefully to ascertain the issues. On nearly all occasions, the blame will either lie with the agent (not advertising it on the best websites, not answering calls, poor photos or description, etc.) or with the property itself. To ensure you have the best agent, it is critical you test them and check your property details against the competition. When it comes to property, the issues are usually down to two things: condition and price. Properties in poor condition can often be harder to let and/or sell unless the condition is reflected in the price, i.e. it is lower than the competition. Highly priced properties can also prove problematic if the expensive gadgets and fancy finishes that go with them are not valued by the target audience – added extras must be relevant and appealing if a higher price-point is to be achieved.

The value and type of free gift you offer will vary according to your target customer. In the rental sector, the offer of a free rent period is very popular. You could, though, be more creative and it doesn't just have to be rent related. How about throwing in a new flat-screen TV? Or maybe even £100 worth of Waitrose vouchers? What about a luxury spa day or a year's free gym membership? In the sales market, you could use top-of-the-range appliances as a focal point in the kitchen and include them in the price, or maybe dress the property and include the furniture; alternatively, you could even gift a cash sum on sale completion. While it may seem frivolous to be offering such gifts to attract customers, when calculated against a potential void or a quicker sale, it's unlikely you'll be out of pocket.

Offering something extra may seem like a marketing gimmick, and maybe to some extent it is; however, every business needs to attract the right kind of customers and get them to sign up. The sooner customers sign up and take your property, the sooner you receive your money. Offering something extra gives you stand-out appeal and a reason for prospective clients to consider your property for longer. Getting into a customer's 'consideration set' is key if you want to make a sale – if you're not considered, you're not going to be viewed, let alone get an offer. Take the time to think creatively and mull over what your customers value – see what extra you can offer and give them that little bit more to make them *your* customer, not somebody else's.

Go For It!

Look around at the different promotions companies offer to get people to sign up. What extra can you offer to make somebody *your* customer?

Rule 96: Expect the unexpected

Understanding what may be an issue in the future can assist you in planning the correct course of action to minimise any problems before they happen.

They say hindsight is 20/20 vision; and it's easy to be knowledgeable about an event *after* it has happened. Of course, learning *after* something has happened can assist you in how you make decisions going *forwards*. However, the best antidote to hindsight is to gain foresight. Foresight is the ability to predict what will happen or be needed in the future – it is the act of looking forwards. While sounding very grand, it can simply be gained by being proactive. When you act proactively, it means acting in advance of a future situation, rather than just reacting to it when it happens. Being proactive means you *make* things happen and take control. In a nutshell: proactive behaviour is anticipatory, or, as I like to say: *Expect the unexpected!*

Proactive management is the most cost- and time-effective way to run your property business. It requires you to identify issues that may arise *before* they happen. Understanding what *may* be an issue in the future can assist you in planning the correct course of action to minimise any problems before they happen. For example, if you conduct a property inspection and notice the carpet looks worn, a proactive approach would be to note a date for the replacement of the carpet, organise quotes and be prepared to replace the carpet *before* it is reported as a repair, or seen as a problem. This approach means you can also plan your finances in advance and ensure you have sufficient funds for the work. Being proactive does not mean you should spend money or do works that are not required, but it is about identifying issues and preparing solutions *before* they become problems.

One of the best ways to ensure you are being proactive is to carry out what I call a 'Property Condition Report'. This can easily be done when conducting your usual quarterly property inspections. The Property Condition Report is just for you and seeks to identify areas of the property that may require work within the next three months to three years. It doesn't have to be anything fancy and can literally be a list of items with dates and action points next to them. For example, 'the kitchen is looking dated – look to replace/update in two years'; 'the boiler is making intermittent funny noises – request engineer to carry out full service when conducts Gas Safe check'. The Condition Report findings should form the basis of any planned works and be factored into your budgeting process. For example, if you are aware a boiler may need replacing soon, it is advisable to start saving a proportion of the rent as soon as you have noted that a potential replacement will be due. This gives you time to prepare the necessary quotes and ensure you have the funds available.

By keeping the Condition Report up to date with every property inspection, it will minimise the amount of surprise repairs that crop up. This also acts as an early warning detector for any bigger issues that may be lying in wait. Proactive management doesn't mean problems do not arise, but it does mean you are more prepared for them when they happen!

Go For It!

Conduct a Property Condition Report on a property. Use your foresight and critically assess what work may become due within the next three to six months, twelve months, and two to three years.

Rule 97: Sh*t happens

*No matter what plans you think you have
in place and what unexpected things you
were ready to expect, one fine day you will
be presented with the unexpected.*

You can reference tenants to within an inch of their life. You can background-check them, visit their previous properties, interview their former landlords, check with their employers, trawl though their credit history, nit-pick their banking habits, talk to their parents, partners, guardians and all the rest of it. You can do everything under the sun; cross every 't' and dot every 'i' along the way, but sometimes sh*t happens. It's the same with supposedly cast-iron sales: they can and do fall through. It's just a fact of property investment. No matter what plans you think you have in place and what unexpected things you were ready to expect, one fine day you will be presented with the unexpected. This is because sh*t happens.

At this point, I am not suggesting you roll over and just accept stuff will happen to you. But I am suggesting you take a more relaxed mentality to the business: because stuff *will* go wrong. Things you planned to happen, won't. Tenants who were meant to pay you rent, won't. Trades people who were meant to fix a problem, won't. Sales that were meant to happen, won't. And it will be up to you to pick up the pieces. This doesn't mean you shouldn't try your hardest to avoid such situations, but you need to cultivate an acceptance that this is the nature of the beast.

Property investment is affected by so many different factors, but mostly it involves dealing with people – and people are prone to going wrong. Even people who seem stable, salt-of-the-earth, ever-so reliable, normal everyday Joes can go wrong. Because sh*t happens in their lives too. And, when it happens to them, they don't always know how to react. Nobody can ever predict how someone else may feel or react when they lose their job, or a loved one. Emotions are not as easy to calculate as the net yield on a property. This is why you need to be prepared for the unexpected reactions and consequential fallout.

Once you have the mind-set that sh*t happens and it is part and parcel of the business, you will feel better. You will understand that not much should be taken personally and that such situations are typically just people being people. The best defence is in knowing they *could* happen and planning for when they do. That means, for example, having a financial buffer in place if a sale falls through, or always having an up-to-date emergency contact for a tenant. People have accidents, people die, people go AWOL, and it's always best to know another person in your tenant's world who you can get in contact with.

Always look to get on with neighbours and exchange contact details. If you are planning to do works, pre-warn them and explain the project schedule – keeping people in the loop lets them know you care. Neighbours can also alert you to any potential issues with a property, which can prove extremely useful should it be empty and awaiting a sale – or tenanted by the wrong sort of people. Having additional 'eyes and ears' on the street is a valuable resource and means you can at least expect more of the unexpected!

Go For It!

Introduce yourself to the neighbours and exchange contact details. Explain to them you would like to be kept informed of any issues with the property.

Rule 98: Be ready for emergencies

The best way to prepare for emergencies is to always have a list, or database, of useful contractors who you can call on at a moment's notice.

As you never know when an emergency may happen, the best way to prepare is to always have a list, or database, of useful contractors who you can call on at a moment's notice. These contact details should be stored in your main mobile phone, and also in another format, in case you should ever need to share the contacts with a third party. A simple list can be created in Word or Excel and emailed to yourself or saved using a facility such as Dropbox.

Some types of emergencies happen more often than others and so it is useful to have two or three reliable contractors for the most typical ones.

The key emergencies in property management are:

- boiler breakdown
- escape of water
- blown electrics
- lost/forgotten keys
- broken window/door.

It is advisable to always ensure your contractor list is up to date; where possible, add further tradespeople to your database to ensure you are covered for most eventualities. Roofing matters and pest control may not be run-of-the-mill emergencies; however, at some point you may well have a call for them, and when you do you'll need them in double-quick time!

Ensure your tenants know who to contact in the case of an emergency. It is advisable, in addition to your details, to provide tenants with contact telephone numbers for key contractors in the event of an emergency. Preferably these contractors should be trusted people who you have worked with previously and who you have made arrangements with in advance. This will ensure any problems are repaired as quickly as possible, minimising any further potential damage to the property.

Unless you live close by, and have the time available and skills required, it is always best to have an emergency contractor as a contact. Tenants should be pre-warned that their telephone number is for emergencies only and that any abuse or misuse of the number will result in a penalty fee being charged. Alternatively, there are insurance providers who offer emergency helpline policies, and these could also be considered, although it is important to check the small print and see what is covered.

Go For It!

Make a list of emergency contacts and ensure you save them in a place where they can always be remotely accessed; for example, via email or Dropbox. Always have details for at least two to three contractors for each type of emergency.

Rule 99: Have a support network

*Property can sometimes feel a very lonely
business, so you should reach out to other investors,
organisations and resources
that can help you.*

Every investor at some point hits a roadblock and doesn't know what to do. Having a support system in place for when things go wrong is critical. Property can sometimes feel a very lonely business, so you should reach out to other investors, organisations and resources that can help you. Legislation and regulations are always changing and you will need to keep up to date with these. There is a huge variety of resources available and it is advisable to make use of everything that is out there – especially given that so much of it is free!

If you have not let a property before and intend to do so now, it is best practice to attend a crash course on how to be a landlord. The National Landlords Association (NLA) runs comprehensive courses that will give you the key information needed to ensure you are abiding by the law. Should you wish to pursue further courses and qualifications with them, these are also available. Some councils also run accredited landlord courses and you should check with your local council if they offer any training days or landlord events.

Even if you are an experienced landlord, it is worth attending annual refresher courses, as laws and regulations are constantly changing.

There are a number of different landlord organisations that have content-rich websites and/or publications that offer practical advice, administrative templates, and keep you up to date with changing practices. In addition, being a member of a landlord organisation can help to offer you a support network should you run into difficulties. Many of these organisations offer telephone helpline support, which can advise you on a wide variety of tenancy matters. A legal helpline may also be available via your landlord insurance policy. This option is an excellent resource and can give you guidance on tenancy and property-related issues, which can be especially useful when you find yourself in a complicated area of tenancy or housing law.

The popularity of property investment has seen an explosion in the number of internet property forums. These can be highly informative, as well as affording you the opportunity to ask questions and contribute freely. As with most things, it is prudent to double-check information and be clear of the source of claimed 'facts'. Many of these sites have a friendly, community feel and offer great insight, practical advice, tips and even friendship to both novice and experienced investors.

Even if you intend to manage a property yourself, letting agents are an absolute gold-mine of information and can provide excellent advice on a range of tenancy, letting and property matters. At present, the letting agency sector is unregulated and so it is best practice to seek out agents who are voluntary members of national regulatory schemes such as ARLA, NALS and the Property Ombudsman. (But do remember to check they really are members.)

Having a support network in place not only makes your life easier, but will also help you to learn and enjoy the process of property investment far more through sharing with others who are in the same business.

Go For It!

Check out the various landlord associations and property forums that are available and join one.

Rule 100: The buck(s) always stops with you

The best thing about the buck always stopping with you is that the bucks also stop with you.

You will have learned from The Rules – and no doubt also from your experiences to date – that investing in property is not a champagne-filled affair with glorious bubbles ever ripe for the picking. And I'd hazard a guess that, for some of you, this book, and your investment career to date, has been filled with a number of disappointments. Things that you hoped would happen, which didn't. Secrets of how to make overnight wealth, which I haven't shared. And longed-for riches, which have yet to materialise.

I'm sorry if you've reached Rule 100 to realise that there *really* are no quick wins and easy routes to make money in this game. But that is the reality of most property investment. I warned you early on: this business can be a pretty hard slog at times.

However, the one Rule you always need to remember, above everything else, is that the buck always stops with you. Any property investment you make is yours to do what you can with. It's yours to make the most of – and it's your bucks that will be paying for it. But the best thing about the buck always stopping with you is that the *bucks* also stop with you. Property investment can and does make an incredible amount of money. It can pave the way to financial freedom and give you a life beyond your wildest dreams.

If you can cope with the challenges of the buck always stopping with you, then you are ready and on your way to collecting the bucks that await you. The journey will probably not be easy, and it's unlikely to be quick. But, if you want to go for the bucks, they're there for the taking. Just remember: the buck, *and the bucks*, always stop with you.

Go For It!

Revisit your financial plans and goals. Are you ready to get going and make your dreams a reality? Now write an action plan for the next twelve months. Plan for success.

BONUS RULE: BE YOU

Investing in property is a personal decision. The properties you buy will mean something to you. Even if you don't actually live in them, they will be a part of your business. They will be a big part of the reason why you are in debt and also a big part of the reason why you have money. How you set up and run your property business is a very personal choice. What you hope to achieve and the sort of life you want to live should be reflected in the type of properties you buy. If you want to ditch the day job, you will be buying a different set of properties to if you want to build a pension pot. I don't like to use the phrase, but it's apt: property is horses for courses.

There is no one-size-fits-all. There is no right or wrong way of doing property investment. Every investor is different and everyone has their own goals and dreams they want to achieve. Investing in property is a learning curve, and you will be forever learning something new, no matter how long or how active you are in the business. That is the beauty of the business. It is an ever-changing and dynamic marketplace that holds new opportunities for all walks of life.

Property investment is accessible to all. You do not need any prior qualifications or years of experience. You *do* need access to some money and the desire to learn and apply your knowledge. You *do* need the wherewithal to run it as a customer-driven business and an eye on how you can make money both in the short and long term.

You need to be comfortable with taking some risks and confident of your decisions. You need to be OK with yourself that you are not always going to win, but that you will learn and grow from your mistakes. Most of all you need to trust in yourself. Other people may say they have the secret formula and the recipe for great riches. Some of that may be true, most of the time it won't be. You need to trust your instincts and follow your business sense.

Lastly, you need to enjoy your investment career. There will be hard times when you wish you'd never ever bought a property. But what will see you through is the bigger goal: it's not just about what you're doing, but about where you're going.

Property does not have to be the *end* in itself; it can be the *means* to an end. It can provide you with the means you need to ditch the day job and do what you love. This life is about you, and about what you want. So choose to make it yours.

And don't be afraid to add your own Rules, or even to bend a few of mine.

Happy investing.

Index